HELLGATE PRESS

WIDOW-MAKERS
&RHODODENDRONS

LOGGERS— THE UNSUNG HEROES OF WORLD WAR II

DORIS WINTER HUBBARD

Hellgate Press

CENTRAL POINT, OREGON

HELLGATE PRESS
P.O. Box 3727
Central Point, Oregon 97502-0032
(541) 479-9464
(541) 476-1479 fax
info@psi-research.com e-mail
http://www.psi-research.com/hellgate.htm

Edit: Kathy Marshbank
Book design: Steven Eliot Burns

LIBRARY OF CONGRESS CATALOGING-IN-PUBLICATION DATA

Hubbard, Doris Winter, 1932-
   Widow-makers & rhododendrons : loggers, the unsung heroes of World War II /
Doris Winter Hubbard.-- 1st ed.
      p. cm.
   ISBN 1-55571-525-7 (paper)
   1. World War, 1939-1945--Economic aspects--United States. 2. Wood products--
United States--History--20th century. 3. Defense industries--United States--History--
20th century. I. Title: Widow-makers and rhododendrons. II. Title.

SD538.2.A1 H83 2000
940.53'73--dc21   00-029596

Hellgate Press is an imprint of Publishing Services, Inc.,
an Oregon corporation doing business as PSI Research.

Some men seek shelter from the rain;
others savor life by unhesitatingly standing in its mist!

— *Doris Winter Hubbard*

Table of Contents

Foreword

A Foreword's purpose is to prepare the reader for enlightenment and enjoyment of the work it introduces. So, it is a privilege and honor to help you learn and love the genus logger and its many species that are the subject of Doris Winter Hubbard's fascinating tale of the life and culture of the community where she grew up.

Doris moved with her parents from Southern California to Sutherlin, Oregon near the end of World War II. Her family settled on an old ranch east of town. She attended school with the youngsters of the men who worked in the woods and mills and women who kept house and worked in the men-short mills during the war. She learned firsthand how loggers worked and played, recognized their strengths and frailties and their need for acceptance as essential members of the community.

Doris learned early that loggers were exposed daily to the physical hazards of working outdoors in the rain, snow, wind and on steep slopes and in the mud. Many of her friends and neighbors lost their lives or were severely injured in logging accidents.

Doris' compassion for the womenfolk of logging communities who had the constant worry of whether their husbands, fathers, brothers or sons would come home after their workday is a compelling part of her moving story. These women were as much the heroes as their men in satisfying our nation's essential wood needs.

Doris' subtitle is *Loggers—The Unsung Heroes of World War II*. She states that these loggers bent the rules, yet bailed out the nation. The wood for the war in many forms—cantonments, packaging, dunnage for ships, explosives and paper—was all vital for victory. And it began with loggers.

It took the Government more than a year after Pearl Harbor to realize that loggers were as essential as servicemen and women and shipyard and aircraft workers to fight a war. Once it did, it used every means to keep timber fallers and buckers, choker-men, donkey punchers, cat skinners and log truckers on the job. When the airplane factories and shipyards raided the woods for riggers, some loggers succumbed to the temptation of the bright lights. When a Congressional Committee was investigating how loggers could be kept busy producing logs, one witness responded, "You might try moving the timber to town!"

In her vivid description of Sutherlin—its stores, sawmills, hotels and taverns, Doris typifies many Northwest communities which based their existence and support on the surrounding timber resource such as Forks, Granite Falls, Darrington, Buckley, Cathlamet and Morton in Washington and Vernonia, Willamina, Lyons, Sweet Home, Dallas, Glendale, Prospect, Selma and Mapleton in Oregon.

Doris skillfully portrays Sutherlin's Jug's Club tavern as the primary social outlet for loggers where a sign invited its patrons to "Do Your Logging at Jug's." It was always thus in the big woods—do your logging in town and your loving in the woods as many talkative loggers were wont to do. Jug's is duplicated in every Northwest logging community—a mighty important place for the clan.

Doris learned so much about loggers and logging that her accounts of what each man does in the woods is colorfully and accurately described. By commenting that if a cat skinner has a tumble he may scramble over the top of his machine and "he can kiss his ass goodbye," she is noting the profane tendency of loggers. But seldom are their colorful expressions blasphemous or obscene. But when a tree falls the wrong way or a choker breaks, you could hardly expect a logger to say "goodness gracious!"

Watching loggers heroic efforts to put the big round stuff into the mills to provide the materials for winning the war gave Doris her incentive to write her epic of their contribution. She deplores the uninformed critics of loggers who were never exposed to them or their activities. It galls her that the Government insisted on increased log production for the war and then failed to acknowledge the response, particularly by small logging companies and their employees. She also recognizes that it was loggers who helped rehouse America after fifteen years when few homes were built because of the Depression and the War.

Her title, *Widow-Makers & Rhododenrons*, entices readers with both the danger and beauty of working in the woods which attract young men to that calling.

Doris' final lines pay loggers a sincere tribute: "These men deserve the applause and respect of a grateful nation. And it is long overdue."

– W.D. HAGENSTEIN
W.D. HAGENSTEIN AND ASSOCIATES, INC.
CONSULTING FORESTERS
PORTLAND, OREGON

Mr. Hagenstein is licensed as a Professional Engineer in Washington and Oregon. He is now and has been since 1938 active in the Society of American Foresters where he served two terms as National President; he was elected a Fellow in 1963. He has been the recipient of many forestry awards and has contributed numerous articles to professional journal.

Introduction

Maybe more often than not, the inspiration to author a book comes from unexpected quarters. The concept of taking on such a grandiose project was certainly beyond my wildest dreams. In fact, it was something to which I'd never given a thought.

My first writing endeavor was on a small scale when I wrote and marketed a brochure detailing my successful experiences with acupuncture. This was in 1984 in Stockton, California, where my family and I had lived for 34 years. After giving my brochure the once over, my oldest son, Ron Winter, then in his early thirties, forcefully stated that if I wanted to write about something, I should write about Sutherlin and the loggers! Having spent most of his life in Stockton, he went on to state that he didn't know such a place as Sutherlin and its rowdy, exciting past existed.

Ron was recalling a visit to Oregon made years earlier when, as a teen-ager, he accompanied us on a trip to take in the annual Sutherlin Timber Days Celebration, and to visit old friends and renew acquaintances. During those two days he was subjected to a lot of reminiscing and reliving of the past, both the fun times and the hard times. Everything he saw and heard apparently left an indelible impression on him. Further, it seems as though he had recently read a feature on logging in the *Wall Street Journal* written by a reporter who, as part of his research, spent several days in the woods with the loggers. All of this piqued his interest. Surprised by his remark, nevertheless I let it pass.

Three years later after returning to California from a high school reunion in Sutherlin, I found myself reminiscing about the boisterous and colorful period in which we all had grown up during Oregon's heyday of logging.

Being distanced by years from that point in time and by miles from the close-knit community had allowed me to gain a new perspective on both. It occurred to me that this had truly been a unique and unparalleled experience far removed from most people's general knowledge.

I remembered Ron's remark. There was indeed an untold story that needed telling about a special time in a special place, and, which, unlike other bits of significant history, had never been romanticized. All the seeds were planted ready to grow into a factual exciting account about virile, individualistic, and fun-loving men, whose lives exemplified courage and perseverance. It would be filled with many anecdotes, some tragic and some comic; it would portray women's roles during this time frame, and would include my memoirs—written in a light-hearted manner—to round out that era. And for WWII buffs, it would be a missing chapter.

But I faced one obstacle: I wasn't a logger and, therefore was devoid of credentials to write about the subject. This held me back for awhile, until one day the light bulb went on: Who better to write about Sutherlin's loggers than me? By lucky happenstance, I was an observer of and participant in many facets of these men's lives outside the workplace. This afforded me unique opportunities to gain insight into their novel lifestyle and brotherhood. And besides, I married one.

What I didn't know about logging and the history of the War, the impetus for the logging boom, could be researched. All the rest was tucked away in my head where it remained dormant after moving from Sutherlin in 1953. Furthermore, I still had contacts in the community who could fill in where I left off. And besides, the author Nadine Gordimer wrote, "… in a certain sense a writer is 'selected' by his subject—his subject being the consciousness of his own era." This era was mine!

As I dug into my research it was a real eye-opener to discover what a critical role the loggers played in winning the War. Not just the loggers themselves, but their workplace: Oregon's massive forests. This was made apparent by the amazing and ingenious lengths to which the Japanese went to torch and send those forests up in flames.

It came as a shock to discover how expendable the loggers were, much the same as the frontline troops. The only difference being in how their deaths were treated as non-events to all except family and friends.

It became my passion to give a dying breed of ordinary men, who were asked to perform extraordinary things, a special place in history. I hope you enjoy the reading as much as I have the telling.

In addition to those listed in the resource/reference section of the book, I would like to thank the many others who took their time to aid me in my research: Ruth O'Neill at the Douglas County Law Library who expended much time and energy researching gambling laws, Butch Culver, Beverly Baimbridge, Bill Baird, Wayne Hall, Forrest Rehwalt, Judge Bill Lasswell, George Luoma, Bud and Vera Holm, Carla Parazoo, and Dorothy Huntley.

I would like to give a special thank you to my husband, Alan, who served as my first editor, and who, I was fortunate, either ignored or never heard the admonition to never get involved with a woman who has more troubles than you.

About the Author

The author, Doris Winter Hubbard, whose maiden name was Price, moved to Sutherlin, Oregon, near the end of WWII, where she attended Sutherlin High School and graduated in 1949.

In 1950, she married "Dode" Winter and they had two sons. After several years spent in the logging business, they settled in Stockton, California, where they lived for thirty-four years.

Beginning her career in Oregon, Doris worked for seventeen years as a legal secretary. She left the law office environment in the early 1970s to become a political activist and to devote herself full time to her position as California State Chairperson and lobbyist for a political organization she helped found. Upon achieving the organization's goals, it disbanded.

Ignoring suggestions that she become involved in politics, she returned to the secretarial work she loved, but this time in the all-too-different academic world. For twenty years she worked as secretary to the Life Science Division Chairman at San Joaquin Delta College. For the first five years in this position, she also taught Legal Office Procedure at nights at a local business college.

Upon her husband's death in 1990, she was hurtled into a man's world of trucks and forced to take over the reigns of a failing trucking business. At the end of three years, with all debts paid and equipment sold, Doris remarried and moved with Alan back to Sutherlin, where she now resides.

Having had several small works published, this is the author's first book.

— PART ONE —

WORLD WAR II AND THE SECOND WAVE OF IMMIGRANTS:
HOW EACH CHANGED THE FACE OF OREGON

CHAPTER ONE

The Call to Arms and Oregon's Gold: Lumber

Widow-maker, crummy, choker-setter, fallers and buckers, gypo: To what particular industry would these terms apply? The only correct answer is logging. Unfamiliar to most outside the logging industry, in times past these workaday terms popped up and permeated shop talk and mundane chitchat daily in Pacific Northwest logging towns.

With a few exceptions, each day's passing finds the usage of those regional words and phrases becoming less common, soon to fade away from most people's recollections.

The logging industry as it was in the mid-1940s and early 50s is a thing of the past. Always prone to unpredictable economic cycles, for decades logging suffered through on-again, off-again recessions. On the heels of this perpetual see-saw, bounded the Endangered Species Act, bringing the Northern Spotted Owl on the national scene along with other environmental and land use laws.

Additional squabbles and issues continue to spring to the forefront, such as prescribed burning versus salvaging of dead and dying trees in our national forests. As further controversies and the resultant environmental restrictions and regulations bubble to the surface, they will work toward keeping the Pacific Northwest in a state of partial paralysis.

A logger today is indeed vocationally challenged. In the climate of the times, anyone setting his sights on logging as an occupation sets himself up to quarrel with his bread and butter. He will find himself disappointed, unfulfilled, and unemployed more often than not.

Whatever a person's stand on logging and environmental issues, past history cannot be changed. Although condemned, earlier excesses were brought about by far-reaching and pressing reasons. These deserve to be examined and understood in light of the times in which they occurred.

Truthfully and fictionally, volumes have been written about the Old West, but few accounts published regarding the remarkable epoch that heralded in the logging boom, the flourishing towns it built, and the way of life accompanying it. In many ways living in Douglas County, Oregon, during this era (spanning part of the Second World War and the 1950s), bore a striking resemblance to the rugged, individualist frontier life that characterized the Old Wild West.

Sutherlin, Oregon professed to be the "Timber Capital of the Nation." This story is a tribute to its indomitable inhabitants who made it happen. Those inhabitants were made up of Okies, Arkies, Californians, and other eager newcomers who poured into the area. To the oldtimers living there, this rush of new arrivals paralleled the earlier influx of Okies into California as depicted in John Steinbeck's *Grapes of Wrath*.

There was a reason for that similarity. Many of these new immigrants were Dust Bowl refugees resettling for the second or third time. They ventured to Sutherlin and neighboring logging towns because their last resettlement failed to ease the grim hardships and heartbreak from which they originally fled. Here, readily available work awaited them—and it paid well. This offered them a second chance to fulfill their aspirations and dreams; to seek the prosperity that escaped them the first time around.

Also migrating to the area were seasoned lumberjacks from the state of Washington. Many of these Washingtonians, or their fathers before them, had earlier migrated to that state from Maine, Wisconsin, or Minnesota. Or they were loggers who opted out and abandoned the dwindling pine forests of Michigan. As opposed to the inexperienced tenderfoots swarming into the area, these men were no strangers to the woods and were swiftly hired for their knowledge and proficiency. By default, however, these experienced loggers were to become the mentors and teachers of the eager wannabes.

Moving on Out

It was early 1945, the war was still on, and Oregon was booming. This boom served as the impetus for my father's decision to pull up stakes and leave Southern California for Oregon's wide-open spaces. Having made an earlier solo scouting trip to that state, he found his ideal property: a small house and a large barn located on 23 acres, seven miles east of Sutherlin.

After Dad's return home from his expedition, mother cautiously approached him with questions. She knew full-well that positive answers were the best she could hope for, since he had already deposited earnest money and sealed the deal to purchase the property. At times when mulling over the move, Dad broke out in an off-key rendition of the then popular song "Don't Fence Me In." The prospect of change appeared to infuse him with a new zest for life.

With gas rationing still a reality, preparing for the trip meant Dad scraping together every precious "A" gas rationing stamp he could lay his hands on. For moves, you could apply for "B" stickers; I'm in the dark as to whether he procured them or not. But, in any event, we managed to get enough stamps or stickers together so we could fill'er up as needed along the way.

Though apprehensive, for my part moving to Oregon held all the seeds of an exciting adventure. But my anxious mother, whose face now wore a perpetual frown, appeared less than thrilled with the prospect of forsaking our comfortable home for a move to, "God knows where."

Our house sold without a hitch, furniture included. The remainder of our worldly belongings—kitchen items, bedding, and clothing—were crammed into a trailer Dad specifically built for the journey. Piled high to the top rail and covered with a tarp, the sturdy trailer was hitched up behind an old 1938 blue Dodge coupe.

Not to be left behind was an inexperienced passenger and family pet, a middle-aged striped alley cat. Her travel accommodations consisted of a slatted wood orange crate placed inside the trunk of the car. With the trunk lid pulled down and tied to the crate top she was assured a plentiful air supply.

Saying good-bye to our old home, we embarked for the great wilderness Mom and I envisioned as Oregon. No sooner had we hit the road than the protesting meowing and howling from the trunk set in. Ruling out other options, however, the cat soon adjusted to the unfamiliar movement of the car and settled down.

The Destination

Located in the Southwestern part of the state, Sutherlin is about 60 miles from the Pacific Ocean. In the late 1940s its business area spanned two blocks, and one of those was only sparsely built upon. Not what could be called a "pretty little town," it evoked more of a frontier image, but set among lush and idyllic surroundings.

The town nestles in a vibrant green valley one mile in width north to south, and the valley extends eastward ten miles to meet up with the foothills of the Cascade Range. When we arrived on the scene, forest after forest of dark green Douglas fir, sprinkled with hemlock and cedar, blanketed the mountains for as far as the eye could see.

It was a noisy and busy community whose population consisted of loggers, mill workers, truckers, and the families of local established businessmen. It became a town composed primarily of young to middle-aged, hardy, robust men and their families, all lured to the area by the work to be found—work that was arduous and hard. As time passed, the logging industry supported the other businesses in town. When logging was slow, the town's economy followed suit.

This was not a place for retirees. Those seeking a time of leisure or recreational activities found no reason to migrate here. Those residents having reached that stage of life were either descendants of the original pioneers, or those lured here from the east in the early 1900s by the prospect of planting orchards and growing bountiful acres of pears, apples and plums that would be processed into prunes.

Other early settlers set about ranching, wringing out their livelihoods by raising sheep and cattle. Turkey ranching also grew to be a thriving activity, and in 1851 Oregon's first turkey farm was established.

Named after one of the early pioneers, John F. Sutherlin, the town incorporated in 1911. Upon our arrival in 1945, according to the census, its population stood at 1301. At that point Sutherlin was only beginning to experience the rapid growth for which the timber industry and the demand for lumber would be responsible. Five years earlier the population consisted of 525 hardy inhabitants within the city limits. With a 147.8% increase in its citizenry within that short time span, Sutherlin was shoved into the limelight for having the largest population increase for any city in the state of Oregon.

Journey's End and Women's Embarkment

Culminating a three-day, slow-paced trip traveling on old Highway 99, then a two-lane highway, we heaved a sigh of relief at reaching the last leg of our journey.

Rounding the corner that placed us on the main street of our new hometown, we were abruptly stopped and detained for road construction. I couldn't believe my eyes! There, right in the middle of the road, hard-hat sitting atop her black hair combed back primly in a bun, stood a young woman wearing flagman's attire. Empowered with authority by the sign in her hand, she animatedly directed traffic around the torn-up street. Having never before seen a woman working at a man's job, I was startled and curiously fascinated by her. As she smiled and motioned for us to proceed on and around the dug-up roadbed, I couldn't resist turning my head to give her another once over through the Dodge's small back window. Without a doubt, Oregon was indeed a strange place.

Before our uprooting, my mother, along with a few of her neighbor ladies, worked at the menial job of packer in an orange-packing shed. I knew many women now worked outside the home, patriotically doing their part for the war effort—but not at a real man's job!

It was just before war's end, and this logging community, as the rest of the nation, suffered from a shortage of men in all occupations. With the departure of men marching off to war, in record numbers women entered into the workplace to take over the vacated jobs. They became crucial to the work force in airplane and ship-building factories. Women were put to the test and found capable of handling the bulk of the demanding jobs inherent in a sawmill. But because of the necessary stamina and rigorous physical demands, with perhaps few exceptions, it was absurd to seriously entertain the idea of women replacing men in the woods—at least in our giant timber area.

Earlier in the latter part of 1942, The Forest Service in New Hampshire jumped on the band wagon and initiated an experiment to determine if the weaker sex could handle the arduous tasks of a sawmill worker. They chose as an experimental station a mill working to reclaim lumber from trees damaged in an earlier hurricane. Women were hired and grouped into categories. They purposely chose dissimilar women distinguished by whether they were short or tall, thin or fat, blonde or brunette, brown-eyed or blue-eyed, or whether they came from farms or cities. It appears the only differing characteristic omitted in the groupings was bust size. Perhaps they slyly calculated in this attribute while charting their statistical criteria; however, it wasn't formally acknowledged.)

WOMEN WORKING IN SUTHERLIN SAWMILL, 1943.
From *West Coast Lumberman* magazine.

September, 1943   WEST COAST LUMBERMAN   19

Women

DO OUTSTANDING JOB IN LUMBER INDUSTRY

Only as a result of the patriotic effort of an army of women, estimated to exceed 6,000, has the western lumber industry been able to maintain production of forest products at a level which has so far met all government demands. Everywhere in Western mills women have taken the place of men now in military service or who now work in other war industries. A few women are working in logging camps. Great credit is due this great army of women which has literally "saved the day" for the lumber industry.

Above: Planing mill crew at the Sutherlin Timber Products mill at Sutherlin, Oregon. Left to right: Effie Peters, Gladys Sands, Anna Bercroft, Dee Rietman, Louise Russell, Rosemary Fishback, Leah Goodman, Edith Bratton, Dorothy Schaich, Josephine Christensen. Below: Mrs. Audrey Bratton, slip feeder on the pond of the Sutherlin Timber Products sawmill.

Throughout the initial test period the women worked only three to four hours per day. From this study, which nowadays would bear the label "blatantly sexist," they reached the following conclusion: After receiving appropriate training, women proved every bit as capable as men in performing the majority of these jobs; that the women's differing physical characteristics had no bearing whatsoever on their individual abilities.

Previously by society's inference, the older women tackling these jobs, including my mother at the ripe old age of 53, would have found themselves relegated to the menopausal junk heap. Suddenly, they acquired heretofore unknown importance and a new found sense of self-worth. They likewise achieved undreamed of independence; yet held the family together while the men were away at war.

Don't You Know There's a War On?

The war that began with the bombing of Pearl Harbor on December 7, 1941, impacted Oregon on a tremendous scale, and irreversibly changed forever the face of this pioneer state. With the rush of patriotic young men enlisting in the armed forces, and the swiftly enacted draft conscripting them from all occupations, there was no time to determine what occupations were—or might become—essential. Nor was there the luxury of time to look ahead and project what shortages of materials might occur because of this loss of manpower. And furthermore, how these shortfalls would detrimentally bear on both the war effort and the civilian population.

"Essential occupations" were defined months later in slow degrees as the actual shortages rose to the surface.

As the war intensified, and nine months after its start, lumber deficits began to impede upon all sectors of the military as well as the civilian population. Desperate not to fall behind, every branch of the armed forces pleaded for this commodity. It was essential to continue with the building of aircraft and ships, and the construction of army bases, which seemed to spring up across the country almost overnight.

There was no end in sight to the skyrocketing demand for lumber, and loggers were critical to the fulfillment of the government orders. For this pressing reason, loggers and sawmill workers in the Pacific Northwest were granted deferments from the draft and urged to increase their production.

On September 12, 1942, the first war order was issued regarding working hours. This edict by the War Production Chief to loggers and mill workers in the Northern States dictated that they immediately begin 48-hour workweeks. For the extra eight hours' labor, the men were guaranteed to receive time-and-a-half pay.

Prior to loggers receiving deferments, much of the experienced manpower was being depleted by the draft and voluntary enlistment. Those remaining to work in the woods were swiftly being lured away by the higher earnings offered in the shipyards and airplane factories.

Shortly after the proclamation regarding working hours, another governmental directive came down. This edict prohibited loggers from deserting their jobs for the more lucrative and less dangerous ones drawing them to the cities. Moreover, to prove the government meant business, a stern warning followed that touched the lives of all deferred timber industry draft registrants. Those men desiring to leave their jobs must prove that their departure would not hamper the war effort.

That mandate fairly well brought to a halt the flight of loggers looking to exchange an ax and saw for a wrench or welding torch. Further, they were forewarned that their failure to support the war effort by refusing to work the mandated 48-hour week would result in loss of deferments.

The next order dished out was a "Work or Fight" order. This applied to all men granted deferments, not only the loggers and sawmill workers.

In the early part of 1943, and a little over a year's time after the first exodus of men from the woods, President Roosevelt reported a six billion board feet deficit in 1942 lumber production. Roosevelt ordered the Chairman of his War Production Board, "…to at once start a program to stimulate lagging production of lumber and other forest products required for war and essential civilian needs."

At this point, the government began to recognize that good forestry practices must be thrown to the wind in order to increase timber harvesting. A representative of the American Forest Products Industries stated that a restructuring of the basic timber depletion provision of the income tax laws was necessary in order to encourage extra timber cutting and log production by timber owners. He stated, "…this may not be good forestry practice, but it is necessary war practice. Forestry practice deficits can be made up after the war. War production deficits cannot: they must be made up now."

Then a severe shortage of pulpwood arose and with it a lack of paper and paper products. Soon afterward a scarcity of newsprint began to surface across the country. This not only affected newspaper publishers, but if allowed to continue, would adversely affect the war's outcome.

The July 28, 1943, *New York Times* reported:

> …cutting of pulpwood has been designated as an essential occupation in notices sent to local draft boards strengthening occupational deferment eligibility of those so engaged.

This pulpwood was additionally used for smokeless powder and containers for shipping ammunition and blood plasma to the armed forces.

Earlier on, the recommendation was made that pulpwood cutters be classed as an essential occupation. According to a New York Times report, the chairman of the House Committee on Brandnames & Newsprint stated, "Subsequently this was done but a little late and slow as they had already drafted much of their manpower."

Further demonstrating the urgency of the dilemma the country found itself wrapped in, the House Committee on Brandnames & Newsprint suggested the desperate measure of using prisoners of war to work in the forests as pulpwood cutters. Lyle Boren, Committee Chairman, said, "Experience has shown that Italian prisoners could be used more easily than German because the latter had attempted sabotage and tried to escape on some occasions."

Subsequently, German war prisoners were used for this purpose in the Eastern United States and proved their reputation for noncompliance. At one point, while at a lumber camp near Harrisville, New York, they decided they'd had enough of this manual labor and went on a two-day, sit-down strike. The Army was brought in to break the strike.

In the Northwest the only known use of prisoners of war in the timber industry was at Fort Lewis Army base near Tacoma, Washington where a POW camp was established. Here they were used in their forestry operations, working only within the perimeters of the base property, which consisted of 86,000 plus acres. Mostly German with a sprinkling of Italian, these prisoners were a compliant group and happy to be there out of harm's way. They planted trees, cut snags, and performed general forestry duties.

Other than this, the proposed grand scheme of utilizing POWs was viewed as impossible to implement in the massive and seemingly endless forests of the Pacific Northwest. The logistics of how they could prudently guard prisoners of war in forests that offered access to thousands of acres of dense woods in which to escape, and any number of directions in which to strike out, was impractical.

It would be touch and go for the guards to watch over prisoners laboring in an insecure environment. Necessity would compel the guards to remain in close proximity to their inexperienced charges, who unwillingly labored in an inherently dangerous occupation. Consequently, the jittery guards themselves stood smack-dab in harm's way. A case can also be made that the very requisites for working in the woods—quick-witted, strong, agile, and fleet of foot—were ironically the ideal attributes needed for someone looking to make a quick get-a-way.

It would be safe to say that in the Northwestern states these were uphill hurdles that proved insurmountable. Affirming this, William Hagenstein, an Oregon forestry historian and writer, active in the Society of American Foresters since 1938, stated that he had no knowledge of POWs ever being used in Oregon. He figured that Oregon loggers would have resisted their use anyway.

Zeroing in on Oregon

Aside from the natural resources Oregon boasted to fulfill the war-born clamor for lumber and wood products, it possessed other vital industries that classified it as a War-Boom State. Portland saw a massive influx of workers who turned up to work in its strategically located shipyards.

In the four years ending in 1943, Portland's population grew by another 90,000 persons. To its credit, by war's end Portland's shipyards turned out a total of 750 ships; this included 322 Liberty Ships and 99 Victory Ships.

Additionally, the availability of cheap electrical power attracted industries such as electrochemical and metallurgical processing plants to the area.

The Japanese recognized the critical importance of Oregon's vast timberlands to our war efforts. Whether it was the state's strategical importance, or as speculated, staged as a morale booster for the Japanese, is unknown. But on the night of June 21, 1942, a Japanese submarine quietly eased in close to the Oregon coast near Fort Stevens and shelled the coastline. Fort Stevens was a Columbia River harbor defense unit situated near the mouth of the Columbia River.

The June 23, 1942 *The New York Times* read:

FOE'S SHELLS FALL ON OREGON COAST
HUNT FOR JAPANESE SUBMARINE PRESSED AFTER MISSILES HIT SAND DUNE NEAR FORT

SAN FRANCISCO, JUNE 22—An enemy vessel, presumably a Japanese Submarine, haunting the shipping lanes linking West Coast ports with Alaska, fired nine high explosive shells in the general direction of Fort Stevens on the Northern Oregon Coast last night, Army sources disclosed today.

All the projectiles, which Col. [Carl S.] Doney, Commanding officer of the fort, said must have been shot from 'pretty far out,' fell harmlessly amid the sand dunes and scrub pine that characterize miles of the coastline just south of the mouth of the Columbia River.

The Oregon attack began at 11:30 p.m. Pacific War Time, and lasted about 15 minutes. Residents of Astoria, to the northeast, and of Warrington [sic] and other nearby points, were aroused from their sleep by the firing.

Col. Doney observed that if the enemy was shooting at the fort his aim was bad. One shell knocked a branch off a tree—the nearest thing to damage that was reported.

Oregon was beginning to get nervous, and rightfully so.

It Glows in the Night

With all households and businesses in the United States scrambling to conform to the blackout restrictions in effect during the war, the timber industry had a case of the jitters as it faced a unique regional dilemma: How to blackout the night-time red glow emitting from every sawmill's wigwam waste burner without snuffing out the fire or causing damage to the burner.

The mills were running night and day, and mill workers labored at a feverish pace in their attempt to close the gap between the need for and the availability of lumber. It was imperative that a solution be found, and quickly.

THE FLOAT PLANE FUJITA AND OKUDA FLEW OVER OREGON FORESTS TO DROP FIRE BOMBS.

It was launched by catapult from the deck of I-25. Upon return, it landed on the sea and taxied up to the side of the submarine. A derrick hoisted it aboard. Partially disassembled and tailplane folded, it was returned to its hangar forward of the conning tower.

Photo compliments of Bert Webber, *Silent Siege-III: Japanese Attacks on North America in World War II: Ships Sunk, Air Raids, Bombs Dropped, Civilians Killed* by Bert Webber. Webb Research Group Publishers.

In Bert Webber's book *Swivel-Chair Logger: The Life and Work of Anton A. "Tony" Lausmann* he tells how this touchy challenge was handled.

> The West Coast Lumbermen's Association called a meeting of the key officials. It was requested that some of the best research men find a way for squelching a wigwam fire without damaging the burner, and also to get a quick start again. Ultimately, an apparatus was put together to produce a "fog" which would damper the fire in about two minutes thus killing the glow but keeping the coals for re-firing—all this without damage to the burner.

The Submersible Aircraft

Unknown to the United States Government, and considered a farfetched impossibility by U. S. Intelligence, the Japanese had ingeniously assembled a fleet of aircraft-carrying submarines, which they designed and built prior to and during the war. On the decks of these submarines they could carry a small seaplane, Yokusuka E-14-Y1 (GLEN) aircraft, enclosed in a water-tight compartment.

The plane required assembly each time it was removed from its hanger and readied for duty. This assembly entailed attaching the wings, fins, and floats, and unfolding the tailplane.

In the early part of September 1942, one of these submarines, I-25, spent several days lurking beneath the murky waters off the coast of Southern Oregon. Held in suspense, the captain and crew awaited favorable weather and a calm sea that would allow them to surface; then hastily assemble, arm, and launch its plane. This pontoon plane, having a top speed of 153 m.p.h., would be armed with two 170 pound incendiary bombs and be piloted by Warrant Officer Nubuo Fujita, the Flying Officer on I-25. The target: Oregon's forests.

Fujita, aware that if his bombing run was successful he could lay claim to being the first enemy to bomb the U. S. Mainland, was fully prepared to die for this honor. In anticipation of his death, he made his final arrangements while awaiting his mission.

In the book *Silent Siege-III: Japanese Attacks on North America in World War II: Ships Sunk, Air Raids, Bombs Dropped, Civilians Killed: Documentary*, authored by Bert Webber, an entire chapter is devoted to Fujita-San. In his own words, he relates his experiences and tells his extraordinary story. While on duty on I-25, he witnessed the bombing of Pearl Harbor, and watched the shelling of Fort Stevens from its deck. Incidentally, Bert Webber's research states that according to Fujita's dairy and the submarine's log, 17 shots were fired at Fort Stevens on the night of the attack. This was confirmed by the submarine's gun crew.

On September 9, 1942, with Nubuo Fujita at the controls, and his observer/navigator, Petty Officer Second Class Shoji Okuda, seated behind Nubuo, the float plane was catapulted from the deck of I-25. His mission: to drop incendiary bombs into Oregon's forests. This was a multi-purpose attack—not only to kindle raging fires, intended to engulf thousands of acres, but to instill fear and panic in the American people and possibly divert U.S.Troops. More than that, it was meant as a retaliation for Col. James Doolittle's bombing raid on five Japanese cities, including Tokyo, which occurred on April 18, 1942.

Making the flight inland, the bombs were dropped about eight miles east of Brookings, Oregon, on Wheeler Ridge. But good old Oregon's rainy weather, plus a misty fog that day, caused the ignited small blazes to die out. What smoldering fires survived were quickly extinguished by a forester, Keith Johnson.

Then again, on September 29th, I-25 re-surfaced. Preparing to make another sortie, the plane was assembled, armed with two more incendiary bombs, and launched inland for a second bombing run. These bombs were dropped in the Grassy Knob area east of Port Orford, but were never found, and no fires were started. The U. S. Government attempted to keep the lid on these bombings, but too many people were involved for it to be hushed.

THE TYPE A PAPER BALLOON

The balloon weighed only 152 lbs.; when inflated it had a volume of 19,000 cubic feet of hydrogen. Its lifting capacity at sea level was about 1,000 lbs. Each balloon envelope consisted of some 600 separate pieces of paper held together by an adhesive made from a potato-like vegetable. Japanese school girls, who had shortened school hours, constituted a large part of the labor force that worked on the paper balloon project.

Drawing compliments of Bert Webber, *Silent Siege-III: Japanese Attacks on North America in World War II: Ships Sunk, Air Raids, Bombs Dropped, Civilians Killed* by Bert Webber. Webb Research Group Publishers.

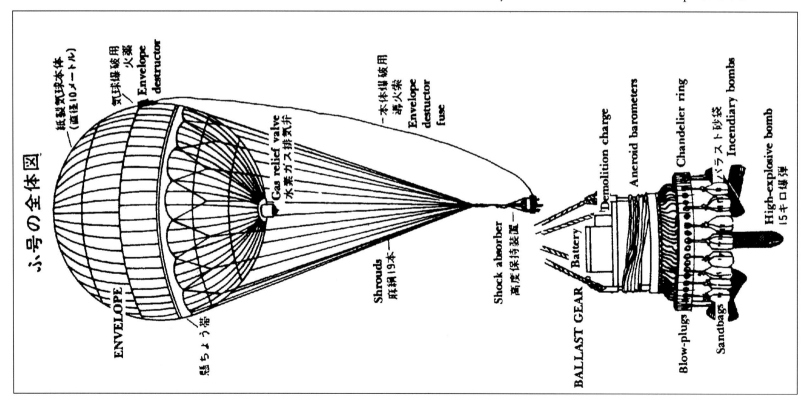

Sounding the Alarm

In Eugene, Oregon, Lt. Col. James A. Framer, a member of an Army party touring the forests in June 1943, affirmed Japanese attempts to ignite forest fires. He warned loggers and mill workers to be on the alert. Col. Framer's mission to Oregon was to initiate a program to train woodsmen as forest protection staff, while at the same time performing their routine duties.

Issuing another alarm, he predicted, "...at 'zero hour' chosen by the enemy, a concentrated attack on Oregon's forests could be expected." He theorized this attack would be by airplane bombing, shelling from submarines, or trained saboteurs.

The colonel delivered a final warning, "that lookout stations might be strafed from the air, and delayed-action bombs might be used to injure fire fighters."

The Balloons

In 1944 a balloon project the Japanese had toiled over for years was being brought to fruition. They were ready to put to the test a hydrogen balloon capable of carrying incendiary devices that could be launched from Japan, then carried on the jet stream to the United States. This barrage started in November and lasted on through March 1945. Their scientists calculated that during this period the jet stream would be the strongest, and the balloons could make their overseas journey in three or four days. Luckily for the United States, this was likewise our wet season, and the damage would be minimal.

On November 3, 1944, the Japanese released the first bomb-carrying balloon to begin its flight towards America. Over the five-month period, approximately 6,000 balloons were launched. After the initial releases, Japanese continued their research and designed their later models with a greater weight-carrying capacity. These could carry aloft both incendiary bombs and fragmentation bombs. Because of wartime news restrictions the landings in North America were kept from the public.

The purpose of this balloon offensive, aside from igniting forest and grass fires and possibly causing casualties, was again to create panic and perhaps divert troops from the war zone back to the mainland. No reported fires were attributable to these incendiary bombs.

The Ill-fated Picnic

The only known casualties from the balloon offensive involved a single incident that occurred on May 5, 1945, on the outskirts of Bly, in south central Oregon. This was barely three and one-half months short of war's end.

Planning to make a day of it, five children, accompanied by Rev. Archie Mitchell and his wife, took off on a Sunday School outing and fishing trip. While walking near a creek, the children and Mrs. Mitchell happened upon one of the explosive-fragmentation bombs and a collapsed balloon. They called to Rev. Mitchell, "Come look at what we've found."

Out of the blue, it exploded, killing all the children and the minister's wife. It was unknown what caused the bomb to detonate; conjecture was that one of the children may have touched or kicked it.

Adding to the tragedy, the surviving families were sworn to secrecy and warned not to discuss it. Various opinions have been put forth as to why the balloon-bomb campaign terminated. Several authorities believe the Japanese abandoned it because they received no reports of any damage caused by balloons—not even any word or rumor that any had successfully landed in the United States.

But the major reason the Japanese terminated their balloon-bomb launchings was because they had no more balloons. B-29 bombings had burned down much of Tokyo, including the balloon factories. In this fire, all 300 of an advanced-design rubberized-silk balloon, which had been returned for re-cementing of the seams, were burned.

In the summer months when the jet-stream changes, the Japanese had planned on launching a larger balloon. But these balloons had also been destroyed by the fire bomb raid, and the rail lines to the coastal launching sites had been blown up.

In the aforementioned book, *Silent Siege-III*, published in 1997, author/editor Bert Webber documented only 361 incidents of the finding and recovery of balloon parts, bombs, and/or bomb fragments. These incidents were scattered from the Aleutian Islands to Mexico and as far east as Detroit, Michigan.

Webber's documentation shows that with 53 recorded incidents, Oregon was the site of the largest number of recoveries. From this, it could be concluded that it was also the site of the largest number of landings.

As recently as 1992, a bomb fragment was discovered at Applegate Lake, Jackson County, Oregon—making it the last numbered incident.

Mr. Webber cataloged all incidents by date and location, and expressed concern over the small number of recovery incidents compared to the number of balloon-carrying bombs launched. With a word to the wise, he notes, "…that list is open-ended on the presumption there are still undiscovered bombs and balloon parts some of which will eventually be found—hopefully not because somebody is killed in the process."

The New Breed

All of Oregon's abundant resources were crucial to the winning of the War, as were Oregon's citizens. Neither's contributions can be underestimated.

Not only were the descendants of the early Oregon Trail Pioneers ready and willing to stand up and be counted, but the new influx of hardy men and women to Oregon seeking work in essential occupations gave their all to the war effort. Together they worked for the good of their country and were united by their patriotism and determination.

The integration of these two diverse groups would eventually cause the courageous, hardy, and steadfast traits of the pioneers to fuse and absorb with the determined and heroic efforts of the new immigrants, and eventually blend to form a distinct culture—a unique new generation of Oregonians.

CHAPTER TWO

The Dark Side of Strawberries

Making a cursory survey of the two blocks that comprised the business portion of town, we headed eastward. For the next six miles we crept along the washboard-like graveled county road, swerving back and forth to dodge the axlebreaking chuckholes. Upon arriving at Plat K, we made a right and drove another mile or so.

Mom and I suppressed the uneasy mixture of anticipation and anxiety we felt as Dad wound up the long driveway toward his Shangri La. Pulling up in front of the house, we were dismayed to find that rather than it being empty as we expected, the sellers were still in residence.

For whatever reason, escrow had not yet closed. Dad explained to the sellers that the realtor had written to him indicating the anticipated closing date, and he acted on that assumption. So there we were without a house to move into or a place to lay our heads.

There wasn't a room in town to rent. I don't recall what dickering transpired between my parents and the owners, an old Swedish couple, all I know is we were granted roosting rights to a dreary abandoned chicken house. This hen house sat a short distance from the main house. The old couple assured us that they'd given the place a good scrubbing after the departure of its last natural occupants. We hoped that included delousing!

Although not too happy with the situation, but lacking other options, Mom and Dad yanked a mattress and cot off the top of the trailer, and I pulled the poor bedraggled cat out of her cage. We set up what, at best, might be called light housekeeping.

We cooled our heels and perched in this chicken coop for a week or so, but for what felt like an eternity while we awaited the close of escrow. It was May, but for Oregon that doesn't necessarily denote Spring weather. In fact, the weather was appropriately foul. For most of our occupancy it rained, it drizzled, and intermittently it poured.

The day following our arrival, Dad made a hurried trip into town to purchase sheets of isinglass, a whitish semitransparent material, that he tacked up over the chicken wire. This helped keep our temporary abode a little warmer. It wasn't comfortable by any stretch of the imagination, yet it kept the colder air out. Being unable to see more than blurry objects outside added to the perception that we'd been plopped down in a gloomy damp cocoon. Since this was Dad's deal, he tried his best to put on a happy face.

My disheartened mother managed to extract from the sellers the right to cook dinner and wash dishes in their kitchen as long as she didn't interfere with their routine. Hunched over plates shakily balanced on our laps, we dined in the hen house and prayed for escrow to close and the sun to shine.

Being cooped up in the chicken house with the occasional diversion of attending to the cat's needs, served to set everyone's nerves on edge. Drearily huddled on our makeshift beds with little to occupy ourselves except playing Rummy, talking to the restless cat, and listening to the dance of rain on the chicken shed, didn't make for the start of a new happy home life. This held especially true for my parents since they had already operated under a mutual truce of several years duration.

Severing the Ties

My parents divorced when I was four years old. For several years prior, they owned and operated the River Bank restaurant, service station, and campgrounds on the Santa Ana River in Southern California. This is now the site of Prado Dam. The hiring of an attractive divorcee as a waitress became my folks undoing. Dad became enamored with her, which led to my parents' parting of the ways.

Shortly after the divorce, Dad and the willing waitress married, and together continued to run the business. During this time I lived with my Dad, new stepmother, and her two children. After a stormy, turbulent five years, they too split the sheets.

All this came about during the Depression. Following my folks' split up in 1936, mother fortunately found employment that also provided a roof over her head. Unlike most women of her generation, prior to marriage she'd acquired a useful trade. Having completed a course of training at Wolfe's Dressmaking and Tailoring College in Kansas City, Missouri, she received her diploma.

Although this diploma was signed in the year 1919, she had no trouble finding work as a seamstress in a cleaning establishment in Los Angeles, about 80 miles away. Inasmuch as part of her wages went toward rent for a cramped cubicle in the establishment, there was no way she could take care of and provide for me.

If women worked at all at that time, they were expected to give it up when they married. Women's true identity was bestowed upon them only upon becoming someone's wife or mother. Not only did divorce throw her back into economic dependency on her family, but being a divorcee, or "grass widow," carried with it a certain stigma. "Good women" looked down on her as flawed and a threat to them. Men considered her an easy target. It wasn't an easy row to hoe.

After his second divorce, Dad warily wrote to mother and extended an invitation for her to come back as, "Doris needs a mother." What he meant was that he'd become frustrated with clumsily attempting to iron my clothes and futilely trying to figure out what to do with my hair. For my part, I was sick to death of rice embellished with evaporated milk and sugar for dinner every night.

Prior to Mom's return, and, I'm sure, with the best of intentions, Dad purchased a new shiny bright electric iron and a small Bakelite radio. To him this was the perfect touch. Money was scarce, and Dad looked quite pleased with himself at having scraped up enough for these "gifts," meant to make her life a little more pleasurable.

Historically, hasn't that always been men's way of atonement for some minor to major infraction or travesty—the presentation of a gift?

For some, a pearl necklace, perhaps a dozen red roses. For my father, aware of mother's practical and prudent nature: a new iron to ease her work, and a radio to fill the vacuum of silence while performing it.

Mother didn't exactly fall all over herself in gratitude, perhaps reasoning (more than likely with justification) that wife number two took the household iron with her. And for that matter, maybe the old radio too. Rather than gifts, these were odds-on replacements that he would have needed to make anyway.

The truth of the matter is that Dad never quite got over mother's failure to graciously thank him for those modern electrical conveniences. After all, he'd been so thoughtful, and they weren't cheap.

Suffice it to say, it was this brand of thinking, though well intentioned, that, no doubt, contributed to the ushering in of the Women's Movement, which men of my father's generation failed to comprehend.

Flying the Coop

On one of Dad's last trips into town to check on the slow-closing escrow, I went along for the ride. Standing inside the real estate office, I puzzled over a sign posted on the wall. It admonished in bold letters "No Caulks!" This same notice was hand-lettered on windows or posted on doors of most every business in town. Unaware of the definition of "caulks," I assumed it to be some strange nationality I'd never heard of or maybe this was an Oregonian word for loiterers or vagrants.

In due time I came to learn that caulks are loggers' boots. These hard leather boots have hobnails and caulks embedded in the soles, which makes a man more surefooted when working in the woods. Considerable and irreparable damage can be done to wood floors or carpeting when callously trampled on and punctured by these caulks.

On this trip the realtor informed Dad that escrow would close the next day, which it did. We finally gained possession of the house and flew the coop.

Only then could Mom and I objectively view and appreciate Dad's purchase, which up until that time we considered his folly. The incessant drizzling rain and the unplanned miserable stay in the chicken house had clouded our vision.

The Spread

The house sat back from the bottom fence line approximately half of the 23 acres. The land in front of the house gently sloped downward, flattening out into open fields. The remains of a tired, neglected and forlorn pear orchard set off to the west. These pear trees appeared to have long ago passed their prime; nevertheless, they continued to sporadically produce sufficient fruit for canning.

The modest house was well maintained and consisted of four rooms and an unfinished attic that became my bedroom. With only a small window at each end of the open attic, I suffocated in the summer after freezing in the winter.

The kitchen where we ate was cozy despite being cramped and inefficient. Two cook stoves came with the house. One was an old electric, and the other an even older woodburning stove. Most women at that time would have thrown up their hands when confronted with the ugly, black wood cooking stove and would have called for it to be hauled away. Mother, however, was able to summon to mind from some time past how to cook on it and bake breads in its intimidating looking oven.

When the weather turned cold, the unsanctioned electric iron, the use of which probably conjured up unpleasant memories, was relegated to a spot high up in a cupboard. Two heavy antiquated flatirons were then withdrawn from storage. She kept these in a constant state of heated readiness on top of the wood cook stove or the wood heater in the living room.

Behind the house and bordered by a white picket fence, was a small-scale garden. Despite her many chores, Mom kept this yard planted with multicolored varieties of seasonal flowers. On the other side of the picket fence a gravel driveway led up to an outbuilding purporting to be the garage.

Situated a respectful distance beyond this, was the nondescript weathered barn. Although this barn had seen better days, it still served the multitude of purposes for which it was built. Here Elsie, the quirky resident Jersey cow negotiated into the purchase price of the place, lumbered in every evening for milking.

The barbed-wire fence enclosing the pasture began and ended on either side of the barn. This lush green pasture butted up to a small knoll covered with the usual scrub oak and dotted with stately Douglas firs. Here and there stood a few large, spreading Oaks, their old gnarly limbs draped with light graygreen moss. As though unfit to mingle with the impressive firs and oaks, a small grove of redbarked madrone trees grew on the far side of the hill near the back fence line.

With the coming of Spring, wild strawberries poked their tiny red heads up and intermingled with the wild flowers growing in the pasture. Thickets of thorny blackberry vines covered a portion of the barbed-wire fences guarding our property, and in the summer they yielded a bounty of delicious sweet blackberries. Braving the thorns, not only did we relish eating them in season, but mother canned them for later consumption in the form of pies and other desserts.

Inarguably, you couldn't have wished for a more unspoiled and serene place to live.

The Shopping Center

Roseburg, located 12 miles south of Sutherlin and the county seat of Douglas County, was the nearest town of any substance in which to shop. For us, since money was tight, the purchase of new furniture and

THE SPREAD
Home property, 1946 (*Top*)
Barn (*Below*)

other needed odds and ends was out of the question. Because of wartime shortages, most household appliances and other everyday items such as sheets and towels were unavailable anyway. They remained hard to get for sometime after war's end. Plumbing and building materials were as scarce as hens' teeth, and a found nail was a prize.

Having abandoned all our furniture in the move, the acquisition of suitable beds and a table and a few chairs were items high on our priority list. Mom did bring her wringer washing machine along for the reason that it couldn't be replaced. If something irreparable went wrong with it, it would have been back to the old washboard.

By way of fulfilling our pressing needs, combined with the desire for a little socializing, on Friday evenings Dad drove us over to the Roseburg auction. Pleasant diversions from the work and solitude were rare, and this Friday evening outing became the highlight of our week.

The Roseburg Auction set on the outskirts of Roseburg, and about ten miles south of Sutherlin. Because of the poorly maintained condition of the county road into Sutherlin, it took a minimum of 45 minutes to drive to the auction from home. Going south from town, you traveled on Highway 99, which, except for a few gentle rolling hills, ran along mostly flat terrain.

In those ten miles, besides passing several small mills, a person could count five large sawmills all spewing burnt sawdust from the wire domes of their burners. These wigwam burners, so-called because they looked like large teepees with softened, rounded peaks, burned day and night. At night, the burning fire was like a beacon and cast an eerie red and gold glow against the darkness of the night sky.

Before entering the small community of Winchester, you had to bravely navigate your car through a tight turn onto the narrow concrete Winchester Bridge. Built some 20 years earlier, this bridge provided transport over the rushing North Umpqua River. Crossing its span, you enjoyed a birdseye view to the east of the Winchester Fish Counting Station. But it was the dazzling blue water tumbling down over the spillway that dominated the scene. This was the termination point of the Winchester Dam.

Looking off to the right you saw the wide expanse of the river making its way onward past the towering Coast Mountains.

The auction building and livestock barn set on about an acre or so of land. This provided sufficient parking for cars, trailers, pickups, and livestock trucks.

I reveled in the flurry of activity, the hustle and bustle of the auction, and mingling with the people as they touched, poked, and looked over items, large and small, to determine their maximum bid.

My parents busied themselves ferreting out and examining boxes containing anything and everything. You never knew what priceless gadgets and stuff might be hidden in a box, so it was important to check everyone. With wartime shortages, the auction was your best bet to find many items that you couldn't get your hands on at a store, not for love or money. Highly prized were plumbing fixtures such as faucets, washers, and odd pieces of pipe—anything that would come in handy to repair or replace old plumbing.

Dad always kept an eye out for tools and all kinds of things that could be used on our place, either for immediate repairs or a future dreamed-about project.

Although money was short, Dad managed to scare up enough so I could buy a coke and soggy hot dog smothered in mustard and relish. You plunked down your money for these at the makeshift counter thrown up at one end of the barn.

The sale of farm animals took place in an enclosed arena, which was encircled by roughly hewn, narrow bleachers where the buyers and bidders sat. This arena sat at the opposite end of the barn. The babble of the auctioneer fascinated me as I watched the varied-colored calves, milk cows, and other livestock being herded in for the buyers' inspection.

The tell-tale signs of the presence of farm animals that cropped up on the straw-covered dirt floor, and the accompanying odor, didn't seem to put a damper on the bidders' appetites. They went right on wolfing down their freshly cooked hamburgers or hot dogs while vainly attempting to fend off buzzing flies.

After loading whatever pieces of furniture, boxes of canning jars, garden tools, or just plain junk the folks had scared up, we headed home.

Once there, the treasure hunt began as they set about eagerly examining the mysterious contents of a few boxes purchased sight unseen, contents unknown, for 25 cents to 50 cents a box. You could be sure that whatever treasures lay inside would be used sometime, somewhere, for something.

Making Ends Meet

Through the methodical acquisition of sturdy odds and ends of furniture, and mother's resourcefulness, the house soon took on the appearance of a home. The beatup kitchen table was draped with oil cloth, the scratched chest of drawers was dressed up with the customary embroidered scarf, and curtains found in a box were altered and hung.

Despite Dad's declaration that only the absolute necessities were to be loaded on the old trailer, Mother had managed to smuggle on board two prized hats and several pairs of gloves. These must have had considerable meaning to her or represented a part of her identity she wasn't willing to leave behind. Mother personified frugality. There wasn't an ounce of frivolousness in her nature. So they surely held a special place in her heart.

But for all that, once those hats, stowed inside sturdy, colorful hat boxes, were stored away at the top of the closet, they never again saw the light of day. At least not until some years later when the hat boxes were pulled down from the shelf and their contents discarded in order to reclaim the storage space.

She was quick to point out to my father that hats were not worn by the women of the town. Nor were there any social events to which wearing a lady's hat would be appropriate. Come to think of it, social affairs were rare unless you counted the Saturday night dance at Turkey Hall in Oakland, an occasional school pageant, or whatever impromptu happening took place in the local bars.

Several local women's clubs, such as the Sew & So Club, met once a month, and for women who played Bridge they might be invited to join the Women's Bridge Club. For the most part, membership in these social organizations was confined to wives of the local established citizenry or businessmen of the town.

For all that, it didn't take long for Mom to adapt to the routine and hard work on the farm. As near as I could tell, she thrived on making do and doing without. Actually, it suited her and her Amish/Quaker background.

The hats soon became mere mementos—just souvenirs of an earlier time, unimportant in the scheme of things as they now were.

The Workshop

After systematically scavenging lumber, then biting the bullet and purchasing the rest, Dad began building a workshop a short ways behind the house. After completion, he put together a covered and partially enclosed breeze way to provide access to the shop from the house. Many an evening during the summer and much of the long wet winter he spent puttering around in his proclaimed domain. He kept busy either repairing something or devising an innovative tool or handy device designed to make work a little easier.

This shop was a lesson in organization with drawers, cupboards and shelves running along all walls. Above a sturdy workbench, he built a solid block holder in which he drilled out slots to hold every size screw driver. A special hole was drilled to accommodate each drill bit.

Every item, whether a flat shovel, a regular shovel, a small saw, a regular-sized saw, or a hack saw, each had a place. And by God, after you used anything, it had better be hung back in its designated spot.

No excuse was acceptable for a tool not being returned to its reserved location. While each tool was suspended on the wall, he drew an outline around it, removed it, and then patiently painted inside each outline the exact duplicate of what belonged there. "Any damn dummy can find the spot where it belongs!"

He operated within his shop as a surgeon in an operating room. Without looking, he expected to put his hands on anything he grabbed for, and there was hell to pay if it was missing. Mom and I lived in dread of misplacing a tool or neglecting to clean it before returning it to its spot.

In one of those crevices or cubbyholes Dad stashed his chewing tobacco, which he chewed either outside the house or in the shop. And stowed somewhere in a hidden crevice within this sacred domain was a fifth of Four Roses purchased when he'd come by an extra dollar or two. Every once in awhile, whenever he deemed it appropriate, he'd take out the secreted bottle and have a little nip. Only he knew what constituted appropriateness. I know his birthday invariably signaled the time for a few slugs. Throwing caution to the wind, more than once he'd assume an "Oh, what the hell" attitude and therapeutically consume what remained of the safeguarded contents, much to my mother's consternation.

The Reality of It

To bring in much-needed income, we spent the first two summers picking string beans in the Roseburg area and prunes on the outskirts of Oakland. Although Californians bear the nickname "prune-pickers," I'd never seen nor held an unprocessed prune. In my mind's eye I pictured them exactly as they came in packages from the store — black, sticky and wrinkled. I was flabbergasted on our first day of picking to see the firm, dark purple fruit hanging on the trees. Delicious and sweet, they possessed an entirely different flavor and texture than dried prunes.

Being a prune-picker wasn't all that bad as you could find relief from the hot sun under the shady trees. But the bean picking is something I don't care to repeat. Standing between the rows of twining vines, it was impossible to retreat from the sizzling midday sun. And any welcoming breeze that might stir seemed unable to find its way down the narrowly spaced rows.

Looking back on the move, I wonder how Dad figured we'd put bread on the table after we settled in. We sure didn't have a bundle of money. Whatever second thoughts he may have had were obliterated by a sense of adventure. Sometimes you just have to say "the devil be damned," and do it! Rural Oregon offered an opportunity to get away from it all and start over. The real economics of the relocation appeared to have been left to chance.

Before selling out, Dad gave up his good-paying job as a guard at Camp Anza near Riverside, and Mother quit her orange-packing job. Camp Anza was one of many hastily built wartime army camps that sprang up around the country.

For the first time in their lives, between the two of them they were bringing home good money and managing to put a little away. After surviving the lean Depression years, having extra money to purchase U. S. War Bonds and still stick some in the bank afforded a certain amount of longed-for security. Giving it up for the unknown called upon a reserve of good old pioneering spirit.

I can only imagine Dad anticipated getting on at one of Sutherlin's many sawmills. However, before this opportunity presented itself, the War ended. The young returning veterans came back to fill these jobs, a few to reclaim ones they left behind.

Nevertheless, a year or so later, because of the continuing clamor for lumber and the corollary building of new mills, labor again became hard to find. Despite his age of 63, Dad hired on at Sutherlin Timber Products. Standing at 6 feet, he was a husky man and in no way appeared his age by looks or by action.

At last there'd be a paycheck that didn't take the labor of the three of us to earn.

The Flood

Our unexpected initiation into becoming fullfledged Oregonian "Mossbacks" or "Webfoots" came about in the midst of our first winter in Sutherlin. Nature gleefully staged for us torrential nonstop rains, making rivers out of streams and sending Sutherlin Creek over its banks. The Sutherlin paper reported it to be the worst flood to hit the Sutherlin Valley in 34 years.

On January 4, 1946, the *Sutherlin Sun* read:

> ...Water covered the valley and surged in a torrential stream down Sutherlin Creek. One citizen rowboated in from east of town. At the height of the flood a newcomer purchased a ranch east of town, even though he was unable to leave his car to look at it.... "Real property in this community is valuable for Sutherlin and Oakland will grow with the lumber industry."

At one point during the storm, with water lapping and swirling about the old Dodge's running boards, we braved our way into town

SUTHERLIN FLOOD 1946
Note the drinking fountain in the foreground.
Highway sign shows the way to Highway 99,
northward to Oakland or Eugene. Rand Theatre later
moved down one block on the opposite side of the street.

for much-needed groceries. Determining where the murky water stopped and the sidewalk began, Dad pulled up and parked the car in front of Culver's Market.

Grabbing our attention as we gathered up courage to lower our shoeclad feet into the muddy water, our eyes were drawn to the second story window above Culvers. Laughing along with anyone who spotted him, a good-humored citizen hung out of the window. Carried away by the moment, he held his fishing pole in his hands and jokingly cast out the line into the obscure flood waters.

We took turns tip-toeing out onto the submerged running board and then wading through the muddy water into the market. Jack Culver, Sr., like several other hearty businessmen, gamely made the effort to conduct business as usual and accommodate townsfolk desperate enough to venture out. Encased in hip boots and standing in two inches of water, Culver worked behind the counter ringing up groceries on the cash register as debris drifted by.

After surviving this flood and the miserable winter just as well as the old-timers, we considered ourselves card-carrying Webfoots. Future winters should be a breeze.

Losing Their Heads

Spring made its welcome appearance despite sporadic rains. Needing a more stable source of income, my parents decided that rather than picking other people's produce, they'd grow and market strawberries. Before they regained their sanity, three acres of berry plants were planted in the flat land that ran below and to the west of the house.

The seller of the strawberry plants warranted them as "Everbearing," and let me state unequivocally, they absolutely came on as being. For the next several years these berries and the plants that produced them became the bane of my existence.

The farm now under way, Dad gave up his mill job with the flawed and misguided intention of living off the land. He bought a couple of calves to raise and graze on the grassy pasture behind the barn; he revamped the infamous chicken house, and Mom stocked it with laying hens acquired as money would allow from our all-around favorite shopping source—the auction.

Mom coveted a small flock of Bantam hens and a rooster put up for bid. With their ornamental gold, flaming-red, and orange plumage, and their funny feathered feet, they were cute as well as comical. Despite failing to fall under the usual category of "functional necessity," but instead "frivolous and amusing," they indulged themselves.

"Cocky as a Banty Rooster" is not an expression without merit, and the territorial confrontation that took place thereafter best characterizes my father's no-nonsense policy. My diary chronicled the rise and fall of the renegade rooster.

> Sat, March 23, 1946: It rained off and on all day but I managed to hoe eight rows of strawberries. The Banty rooster jumped on Daddy and dug his spurs into Daddy's hand and made it really bleed.
>
> Thurs., March 28, 1946: This morning Daddy cultivated the runners and I started picking them up but it started raining so we put some strawberry flats together.
>
> Daddy chopped the rooster's head off today.

Blowing his second chance, the rooster's reign of terror came to an end. The Stay of Execution became invalid and the original threatened sentence was carried out.

To make the farm complete, Dad set upon another hairbrained and irrational plan of action—to plant several acres of wheat and barley. After all, the land set idle while taxes accrued.

Let me mention that the planting of these crops was accomplished by plowing with a Bearcat tractor. Its name turned out to be incredibly appropriate. Not your customary sitdown, lean back, ride-along tractor, rather it was a large garden tractor that you walked behind. Instead of rubber tires, the wheels had metal cleats.

The only weakness to which Dad admitted were his aging knees, which swelled up and became painful when he spent a hard day on his feet. It wouldn't take much of this tractoring to lay him up, so we spelled each other at trudging behind it.

To operate this chugging monster called for considerable strength and a strong back. It was no picnic to handle at its best, but with the plow attached and embedded in six inches of wet, clay-like soil it was darn near unmanageable as it inched along.

Of all the jobs I inherited by virtue of being an only child, this proved the most physically demanding. Anticipating this, Dad, for the first time I could remember, looked almost apologetic as he questioned my ability to maneuver the punishing machine. I knew he couldn't plow that field by himself, and this was one job mother couldn't give him a hand with. I assured him I could manage it.

Plodding over the uneven ground behind that hellish pitching tractor, wrestling with it and struggling to hold it steady and upright to plow a furrow, twisted and wrenched your arms and back. This in turn put a tremendous strain on your legs and knees.I know this must have caused Dad a good deal of pain.

This kind of laborious plowing of several acres of uncultivated ground was in actuality beyond the prolonged capability of a garden tractor, and, I might add, the poor soul expected to be at the helm. The following season Dad got his head on straight and hired a man with a farm tractor to do the work for a share of the crop.

Although my parents displayed little affection toward each other, they coexisted within civilized parameters with only occasional breaks in their truce. My foggy perception of the situation had me believing that we had a good time at whatever we took on. I guess I failed to recognize how miserable I should have been because no one bothered to point it out.

Time Out

Despite the incessant rains, I looked forward to the approach of winter and my subsequent unemployment. School occupied most of my time, and what work remained undone, my folks could handle.

In spring and summer, especially at the peak heat of the day, we found time for more pleasurable pursuits. Mother occupied much of her free time sewing—mostly school clothes for me. I hated to admit that Mom made my clothes. It was a dead giveaway that we couldn't afford store-bought, not even out of the Sears catalog. She had to squeeze every penny just to buy the material. If I pointed out something I especially liked, Mom took in all the details, then made her own pattern. After cutting out the dress, she headed for the old treadle sewing machine.

Being a typical unappreciative teenager, it never occurred to me that rather than feeling ashamed of my homemade clothes, I had bragging rights to the fact that they were one-of-a-kind, designed and sewn by a certified professional seamstress. What few clothes she could afford to make were beautifully tailored with perfect seams. When it came right down to it, most people in town looking for a special outfit couldn't afford the services of a person like her. But, regretfully, I never sang her praises, nor passed on any compliment I received. I don't even remember if I said thank you.

What I do remember is the nylon parachute that she converted into multi-tailored blouses, dresses, and slips.

It was right after the end of the War when Mom, thumbing through a magazine, saw an advertisement offering government surplus parachutes for sale. For a nominal price, the buyer would receive one parachute from which she could recover yards and yards of white nylon material.

I have no idea how many yards went into the making of a parachute, but Mom spent days and days ripping and tearing it apart. No easy task when you consider the number of extra-sturdy seams it took to put one of those together. She even salvaged the nylon thread that she ripped from the parachute, at least the pieces long enough to make it worthwhile.

I ended up with a white nylon blouse that buttoned down the front, a white nylon slip-on blouse that buttoned in the back, both longsleeved and shortsleeved, and several nylon slips. I begged off anymore. One thing for certain—none of this clothing wore out. The best you could hope for was to outgrow them.

Still, the white nylon wearing apparel was one step above the floursack dresses many of us girls wore during the Depression. The rugged cotton material for this frock-of-the-month came courtesy of commodities handout. Things were looking up with the recycled chute.

On dog days when it was too hot to work, I plopped myself down on the couch with the latest movie magazine bought on the last trip into town. I couldn't wait to catch up on the contrived fantasy doings of movie stars such as Ginger Rogers, Joan Crawford, Frank Sinatra, and Ava Gardner. I fantasized over the storybook marriage of the blissfully happy Hollywood newlyweds and believed every word of it. I'll admit I did have a little trouble trying to figure out how Louella Parsons sat in on the Hollywood couple's loving, intimate moments that she reported in such vivid detail. Or how she overheard the one-on-one conversations, which she repeated word for word.

Up in my room, the current secreted copy of *True Confessions* awaited my scrutiny. Retreating up there, away from the disapproving eyes of my folks, I gobbled up those torrid tales about lost loves, the lovelorn, and the lovesick. This drivel left much steamy sex to the imagination, but that was OK as mine was finely tuned.

The Sighting

Many a day when no work demanded our attention, I'd whistle for Blackie, a German Shepherd mix, and set off into the woods that to the eye had no ending. With no particular destination in mind, it was easy to lose track of time in a place that gave the feeling of having no connection to it.

The woods were a wonderland filled with varied large and small ferns and luxuriant green undergrowth protected by the thick canopy of trees. Even though it was summer, the many damp spots along the way clued one in that the moss-covered soil was unaccustomed to the warmth of the sun's rays.

Several places along my route I'd emerge from the dim light of the woods into a sunny clearing where sheep lazily grazed on a thick carpet of tender grass.

In heavy rainfall years, the water ran off the hills in mini-streams and oozed out of the ground with each step. I roamed until it was time to turn tail and hustle back home before nightfall.

I especially loved to wander through the woods on warm drizzly days absorbing the sights and smells created by the rain as it bathed the woods with cleansing moisture. It transformed into a magical world of emerald beauty.

I'd heard that rhododendrons grew wild in the forests but had never seen one. On my hikes, I kept a sharp eye out hoping to catch sight of a flowering bush. It would seem that my treks through the woods had failed to coincide with their blooming period, that is until one special day.

Meandering through the forest, a person becomes mesmerized by the surrounding mixed palette of green. Only the varied browns of tree trunks and snapped twigs provide a contrast. When I unexpectedly happened upon a rhododendron bush in full bloom, I couldn't believe my eyes. The fantastic rounded pink clusters, so large and stunning, rested like jewels against the background of darkgreen leathery leaves. At that moment I felt as though I'd stumbled upon a long sought-after treasure.

Whenever encouraged to close my eyes, let my mind wander, and envision myself in the most beautiful, restful place in the world, this is the place to which my mind returns.

Spittle Bugs and Others

Hopelessly held captive on the place for the first two summers, I resigned myself to keeping my nose to the grindstone. Inasmuchas the sale of strawberries provided our main source of income, I became a victim of their prolific production.

The picking season began sometime in May, and the meaning of "stoop labor" hit home. No one asked me, "Do you think you can help?" or "Would you mind?" I heard no promise of, "If we have a good year, we'll see about giving you twenty bucks or so." When your efforts help put food on the table, few pleasantries are exchanged; little money exchanges hands between family members.

Picking started at daybreak. On chilly, frosty mornings, the crisp air stung our faces and finger-numbing moisture covered the plants and berries. Mom placed a pan of hot water just inside the kitchen door. When my fingers turned blue and began to ache from the cold, I headed for the kitchen and plunged my hands into the then tepid water. The warm tingle reassured me that my stiff fingers weren't permanently damaged.

Besides picking the ripe berries, the narcissistic plants required some form of constant looking after. Like a homely, demanding mistress, they wouldn't let you off the hook; they wore you down with an insatiable need for attention and devotion.

After school that first fall, I'd return home to the endless hoeing. By the time the obnoxious weeds had been chopped out of the last row in the patch, they were resprouting and overtaking us in the first-hoed row.

I couldn't get a paying job fast enough to get the hell out of those strawberries. It wasn't just the picking and hoeing. The plants put out runners that needed chopping off. Then enter the ever-present root weevils that devour the plants from the bottom up. A glob of bait sprinkled by hand into the crown of each plant supposedly took care of them. This home-made bait consisted of sugar and an insecticide mixed into sawdust.

Just about the time you let your guard down, the spittle bugs show up. These tiny green insects sit inside a cocoon of what resembles spit and spitefully cut through the stems. Once the stems are severed, the ripening berries dry up.

And don't overlook the usual infestations of slugs, earwigs, and ants that become contenders for their share of the bounty. And the birds enjoyed feasting on them.

Because we depended on strawberries for our living, we didn't eat the nice big juicy ones meant for market. It was strictly forbidden fruit. The ones that ended up on our table were the partially insect-devoured berries and the misshapen mutants.

The Misery Whip

Then, of course, there's the time-honored, proverbial tale of the woodshed. Too old to be taken behind it, we developed a cozy, although antagonistic relationship. Its mere existence suggested a diabolical purpose. Rumor has it that you get a warm, secure feeling from seeing it stacked to capacity with slow-burning, warmth-giving firewood.

My warm glow came about from helping to unload many cords hauled home from one of the mills. But what really made me rosy-cheeked was my introduction to the working end of another implement of torture: an ancient, rusty, crosscut saw. Dad, in a moment of madness, made the high bid on this at the auction. More than likely, his was the only bid!

Not being blind when he purchased this relic from the Dark Ages, I'm certain he understood it took two sets of strong arms to make it work as intended. Old-time loggers appropriately named this saw a "Misery Whip" or "Lumbago Breeder" with good reason.

Nature, playing the role of advance man, managed to have a few large limbs snap off from the immense oaks or apple trees, or caused an aged gnarled oak to fall. By these deceptive means, Dad managed to recoupe his investment.

Light at the End of the Tunnel

All told, my parents bit off more than they could chew. Both on the far side of middle age, they were tired of fighting the endless strawberry-eating insects and the back-breaking work.

Being as how Sutherlin and the surrounding areas suffered from such a severe housing shortage, Dad finally hit upon an idea for a steady source of income. Putting his latent accomplished carpentry skills to good use, he built three rentals on the property.

No doubt, he saw the writing on the wall: Doris, not entirely brain-dead, had no plans to hang around any longer than absolutely necessary, despite being one of those spoiled, only children. (Whenever anyone hit me with this lame-brained, oafish stereotype, I smiled sweetly and nodded. What I wanted to do was set their hair on fire!)

But alas, the time was at hand for me to become sickeningly familiar with the hammer. Nevertheless, I managed to escape before the raising of the third cabin. All three cabins consisted of two good-sized rooms, with the kitchen occupying the same space as the living room. An architecturally perfect outhouse stood a polite distance from the rental. Each cabin set far enough apart from the others so as to afford the occupants sufficient privacy.

By word of mouth, these cabins were rented long before completion.

At long last, this better use of land and resources afforded them a dependable and steady source of income.

In the end, Dad's dream of the good life in rural Oregon was a pipe dream. It turned out to be rather like attending a long anticipated picnic and being served flat, warm beer and rancid, cold popcorn.

CHAPTER THREE

School Daze

Sick to death of the isolation and work at home, I couldn't wait for the start of school that first fall. My Freshman class (all 39 of us) included a lot of nervous and anxious newcomers like me. Beverly Nicolazzi came from Chicago, and both being new on the scene we sought out each other's company. Her Dad and uncle opened a service station optimally located on the busiest corner in town, which was also Highway 99. Before long, I became a frequent overnight guest in their household.

Several students originated from the state of Washington. A son from the newly arrived Amorde family represented the state of Wisconsin. Opal Welch. like myself, hailed from Southern California, her Dad following the rumor of work to be found in the area's sawmills.

The Firman Brothers, Dick and Donald, showed up for school that first day strictly by a quirk of fate. Their family was making a beeline further north for work when the old car gave up the ghost. Just about broke, repairing the car was out of the question. Since this was the way the cards fell, they had little choice but to stay.

Patsy Wahl, a cute and vivacious girl, held the distinction of being a local. Her father, Hugh Wahl, owned a small sawmill outside of town. Community-minded, he made time to serve on the Sutherlin School Board.

In 1933, and down on his luck, Hugh Wahl settled east of Sutherlin at a wide spot in the road called Nonpareil. Here, he found a decent house to rent for $4.00 a month. Through hard work, perseverance, and foresight, Hugh grew to become a self-made millionaire. Being one of only a handful of entrepreneurs to make it big in the county's timber industry, he acquired his fortune at a time when a million dollars was beyond most people's wildest dreams.

HUGH WAHL
Sutherlin's self-made
millionaire and member of
Sutherlin's School Board for
a term in the late 1940s.
*Photo compliments of
Patsy McCoy.*

SUTHERLIN HIGH SCHOOL
Photograph taken in 1949.

Several boys in school came from established families who owned and operated family businesses in town, such as Holgate's Sporting Goods & Gift Shop, Musgrove's Hardware, and Culver's Market.

The Center of Learning

The school building that sheltered us can best be described as a simple, white, two-story, clapboard box. The townspeople proudly erected it in 1911, the same year the inhabitants voted for incorporation. Unimaginatively perfectly square, it consisted of a first and second floor and a basement. About three feet of the basement protruded above ground, which allowed for the placement of small ventilating windows. Altogether, there were nine classrooms: five on the top floor and four, plus the restrooms, on the bottom.

Sufficient light and ventilation for the classrooms at the front of the building came through four sets of triple side-by-side, double-hung windows, two sets upstairs and two downstairs. An equal number were symmetrically installed in the back. Since the two sides of the building were devoid of doors or entryways, four framed-in sets of five-paned windows were placed in each outer wall.

Architecturally, I believe the building represented the Prairie Box or Foursquare style construction popular at the time of its construction. In the front of the building, wide stairs led up to the covered first-floor porch. These stairs and porch were the only redeeming features that saved it from looking like a boring cube. Large double doors off the porch afforded entrance to the school.

The principal's office looked out across the second story porch over the entry. This small, narrow veranda with its white picket-type railing supplied much-needed architectural interest to the old square box.

Perched atop the school, an old traditional belltower embellished the roof line. This housed the now dingy and mute school bell whose pealing in times past had heralded the beginning of another school day.

An easterly tilted flagpole stood off to the right of the front steps in such close proximity to the building that it appeared to be attached.

The Topsy Turvey Campus

This center of learning obtrusively occupied a large lot situated amongst the older residences of the town. Because of limited space, there was insufficient room for anything resembling a school yard. A well-worn and compacted area of grass struggling to survive at the entrance to the school served as a lawn. Running through the center of the grass, a concrete walkway led from the sidewalk to the front stairs.

The old wooden gymnasium used for regularly scheduled gym classes also functioned as the auditorium and assembly hall. It filled the bill for all other extracurricular activities. The basketball/volleyball court took up most of the inside area. Staggered-height wooden bleachers set off to the right of the court. They did duty for seating fans as well as ticket buyers to other events.

Beyond the ball court towards the back, an elevated stage dominated the room. Here school plays were put on and graduation ceremonies held. The restrooms/dressing rooms were at the front of the gym, just inside the doors and to the right.

These facilities served the community well, but there was a major fly in the ointment. The gym inconveniently sat on Central Avenue, four blocks from the school. Sufficient time had to be scheduled for students in each gym class to hustle from school and reach the gymnasium on time. The football/baseball field was located another block east of the gym.

This hodgepodge of nerve centers might be laid at the feet of the original founders, but in all fairness it wasn't their short-sightedness that created the problem. When the school was built in 1911, the population stood at 455. Almost three decades later, the census reported an increase of only 70 inhabitants, not exactly a rapid and uncontrollable population explosion. Those arrivals could easily be attributed to a stable birthrate, not an inflow of immigrants.

The Squeeze

That first year of high school the bottom floor of the school overflowed with 5th through 8th graders. This over-crowding resulted in one elementary class being shuffled off to a nearby church. The high school students, comprising grades nine through twelve, were shoehorned into the limited space on the top floor.

In 1945, nine students walked across the stage to receive their graduation diplomas, whereas our freshman class boasted more than four times that number. This put the squeeze on a school ill-equipped to handle the continuing rapid influx of children moving into the area.

At the start of our sophomore year, more lively new arrivals registered in all classes. The dress fad of the day brought forth boys sporting crewcuts and dirty corduroy pants. The girls showed up in skirts and sweaters with matching bobby socks shoved into saddle shoes.

Two new kids on the block showing up in our class were Joan Powers, whose father opened a barber shop in the hotel building, and Barbara "Bebe" Grabow, another replanted Californian. Moving here from Oakland, Bebe's dad took up residence in Sutherlin to become the town's sole medical practitioner.

Each new school year saw an increase in enrollment in all classes. The logistics of how the school hoped to operate caused the students little concern. Yet there is no denying that our teachers worked under the most unenviable conditions and hardships. Not only were the classrooms over-crowded, but under-budgeting made matters worse.

Shelterless in Sutherlin

Another stumbling block stood in the way of new teachers from out of the area who came to Sutherlin to pursue their chosen profession. Suitable, or for that matter unsuitable, housing or other accommodations were impossible to find. Sutherlin's weekly newspaper routinely published a plea for residents having an extra room in their home to rent it out to a needy teacher.

About the worst misfortune that could happen to a fragile soul was the unsettling experience of being obliged to seek shelter in one of the tiny, dingy rooms in the Sutherlin Hotel. Many unattached and transient loggers now called this place home, and the rooms offered few discernible amenities.

But woefully, this tragic fate befell several of our less fortunate teachers. It would be safe to say that this once-in-a-lifetime experience became indelibly etched in their memories. For years to come, it would provide them with material for hilarious and unrivaled tales.

One of these hapless, unsuspecting teachers was Mrs. Marjorie Leonard. She, in all probability, required the passage of several years' time for the wounds to her psyche to heal. In the long run she, no doubt, could reflect back upon her tour of duty in Sutherlin with some semblance of fondness and humor.

... a Place Like This

> The teacher who walks in the shadow of the temple, among his followers, gives not of his wisdom but rather of his faith and his lovingness."
>
> "If he is indeed wise he does not bid you enter the house of his wisdom, but rather leads you to the threshold of your own mind.
> *The Prophet* by Kahlil Gibran.

In 1949, Mrs. Leonard appeared on the scene as one of the new teachers. She was a pleasant woman in her late forties/early fifties, with a figure that the young girls could envy. Her brown hair, sprinkled with gray, had been pincurled into waves that encircled her head.

Plastic-rimmed modified cats-eye glasses, popular at the time, balanced atop her nose. She could not be called a pretty woman as her face was rather long and thin, and the elongated glasses only accentuated this feature.

Mrs. Leonard was a refined and gentle woman. Her carriage and manner gave reference to a genteel upbringing. All in all, her demeanor and style of dress indicated that nothing in her background could have prepared her for the uncultured lifestyle and mish-mash of students she confronted in Sutherlin.

Always meticulously dressed—perhaps overdressed—for the area, Mrs. Leonard could have made the transition from classroom to a night on the town without a change of clothes. Her extensive wardrobe included many beautiful dresses and complimentary shoes. In fact, she didn't seem to identify with less casual clothing. Or perhaps, because desperation had driven her to spend the week in Sutherlin's hotel, she didn't have the money to squander on more appropriate clothing.

Her writeup in the yearbook stated that prior to her move to Sutherlin, she held a teaching position at U.C.L.A. Here at S.H.C., she hired on to teach English, Speech, and Drama. Additionally, she received the obscure assignment of directing both the Boys' and Girls' Glee Clubs.

The yearbook noted that she and her husband maintained a home in Eugene, 60 miles to the north. Certainly, it wasn't some fanciful whim that led her to desert her home to pursue a career in this rough-and-tumble town. I can only presume she must have fallen upon hard times or become overwhelmed by family problems.

This gentle soul came to Sutherlin determined to instill in us some semblance of culture—in other words, to make silk purses out of sows' ears. In that our student body was a patchwork of backgrounds, she had her work cut out for her!

Determined to widen our horizons, she nobly sought to offer us a glimpse of other realities unfamiliar to most of us. On more than one occasion during music class, she animatedly entertained us with tales of a famous and highly acclaimed operatic baritone. She implied that this friend of both her and her husband visited their home on a frequent basis. The operatic solos that rolled off her tongue were a far cry from anything in our repertoire.

Taking it on the Chin

Inasmuch as Mrs. Leonard failed to take a firm hand in her classes that first week of school, the scales were tipped in our favor. English class presented the biggest problem for her, particularly with the boys. They exploited her indecisiveness many times by being rude and obnoxious. Not being born yesterday, she managed to turn things around by showing overt favoritism towards them. They smugly enjoyed the special attention and she got what she wanted—a smattering of respect.

One dreary, drizzling morning at the beginning of English class, Mrs. Leonard stood at the front of the classroom looking tired and haggard. The signs of sleep deprivation showed on her face. We could sense she wanted to get something off her chest before getting into the conjugation of verbs.

Struggling to maintain control, she exclaimed, "I just don't know how much longer I can stand it!"

Our knee-jerk reaction, with good reason, was that she meant us. At that moment, she held our undivided attention.

Then she squeamishly began to tell us that her life was being made miserable by some ugly, horrid black bugs. It seems as though these insects, playfully vying for her attention, scurried about her hotel room during the night. She feared finding them taking a nap or breeding in her bed when she turned back the covers. Gritting her teeth, her voice betrayed disgust as she admitted that these crawly things were making her crazy. She was at wit's end.

Whether several of her pet boys volunteered or she solicited the favor, I don't know. But, as it was, for the next couple of weekends, after she lead-footed it out of Sutherlin for home, a few boys staged a bug patrol of her hotel room in her absence.

It seems this search and destroy raid was fairly successful, at least until invading reinforcements waged a new campaign and charged under the door from a hidden staging area. But her combat-ready troops remained on standby and were mobilized back to the battle front.

As part of her music and drama teaching chores, Mrs. Leonard was charged with directing our annual Christmas Pageant. This proved to be the moment of truth when we, at last, fell in line.

But, what part of her stamina, sensitivity, graciousness, and sense of humor hadn't been laid to waste in her three-month residence in the hotel, we wrought asunder with rehearsals for this pageant.

As Christmas neared, she jumped into plans for the pageant and got caught up in holding auditions. At least during these evening auditions, she had a place to be other than the hotel.

The Adoration would be held on the stage of the gymnasium. A good turnout of parents and townsfolk could always be expected as few other Christmas activities would distract from our production.

Seating for these types of events was accomplished by filling the gymnasium with wooden, slatted folding chairs. These were aligned in rows across the basketball court. Sufficient room on both sides of the seating allowed for aisles.

Mrs. Leonard put all her heart into making this pageant a success. She came up with the novel ideal of combining the Boys' and Girls' Glee Clubs, and our primary role was to provide musical background for the play. This called for us to line up in two rows clear at the back of the stage.

Numerous evenings of inattentive rehearsal had already exacted its toll on her fragile emotional well-being. Nearing the evening of the performance, and about at the end of her rope, we unwittingly broke down the last remaining scrap of control she could muster.

After deliberately flubbing lines, performing whatever imaginative antics we deemed necessary to elicit uncontrollable giggles from our fellow classmates; singing off-key with an occasional well-delivered belch; and dreaming-up and acting-out blatant shenanigans to distract those trying to recite their lines, we managed to create chaos out of her play.

Her face betrayed her anguish as she pleaded, "Please! Please! Please!" for the umpteenth time and banged her baton on the music stand until we thought it would snap in two. A distraught Mrs. Leonard, wringing her hands, abruptly turned around and collapsed in hysterics on the nearest chair. Placing her head in her hands, she broke out in uncontrollable sobs.

Stunned silence fell over us like a black cloak. We were struck dumb that we'd reduced her to tears and heaving sobs. Rehearsal ceased that night. Gathering in a couple of small groups and whispering amongst ourselves, we drifted out of the now-silent gymnasium. The sound of her inconsolable weeping assaulted our ears and filled us with shame.

We were rowdy and boisterous. We were funloving and high-spirited. We were brimming over with boundless energy—and we were rude. But we were not cruel!

After a hurried consultation amongst ourselves, we acknowledged that she'd bent over backwards to show us respect. Once we thought about it, we knew she was fond of us. Giving her all to make the play a big success, she wanted to tease the best out of us.

Repentant and sorry, we vowed to change our ways. I'm unaware whether any of us offered an apology to our drama coach and choir director, but the next evening we drew in our horns. We blossomed into the melodic, operatic singers and angelic performers she yearned for.

In aspiring to expose us to the arts and bring a little musical appreciation into our lives, she'd made two mistakes. Her first was creatively combining the Boys' and Girls' Glee Clubs. The stage was not very large, and 45 sets of hormones were squeezed shoulder to shoulder in a confined place. Mixing students from different grades might have worked someplace else, but in our close-knit school, we saw few unfamiliar faces. Despite age differences, we knew each other at least by name, face, or reputation.

Her second mistake was positioning this rag-tag choir at the back of the stage at the same time the cast was intent on rehearsing their lines. Adding fuel to the fire, she sought out two of our recent devil-may-care graduates to handle the lighting and stage decorations. Making the most of their talents, they demonstrated that happiness is a bright spotlight gleefully cast on Anna Lou's bosom!

True, the blame could be laid at our feet for exhausting her rationed defenses. Unbeknown to us, she already teetered on the brink.

Although thoughtful parents extended occasional dinner invitations to their homes, and she received friendly support from her colleagues, it didn't compensate for her day-in and day-out miseries. Being forced to live out of a suitcase over a long period of time taxes anyone's patience. This, compounded by unwillingly sharing her dreary hotel room with a form of insect life that aspired to set up light housekeeping, was enough to depress a stout-hearted, insensitive clod.

These intolerable hardships mixed in with whatever family problems she faced all worked to finish off what remained of her mental health. Our antics panned out to be the proverbial straw that broke the camel's back.

After all was said and done, this tireless and inspired teacher, working with muslin thread, wove her silk purses. A transformation took place. On varying Sundays thereafter, we were invited to stand in as the choir at diverse churches in the Sutherlin, Roseburg, and Eugene area.

Further proving that she'd managed to infuse a trickle of refinement into our unrefined and boorish veins, we willingly, without coercion or bribery, purchased tickets for a performance of "Hamlet" in Eugene. For those unable to come up with the price of admission, someone always stepped forward. These kinds of individual helping hands came from behind the scenes. Repayment was never expected.

We piled onto the school bus for the trip to Eugene, and, at the time, didn't realize how privileged we were. Laurence Olivier starred in the leading role.

Culminating the year, Mrs. Leonard proudly put on an operetta with her now-inspired and willing troupe, for which she received well-deserved accolades. The pride she felt at accomplishing her mission, I would hope compensated her for the misery she suffered. By steadfastly aiming for her set goals, she gained a smidgen of immortalityat least with her Sutherlin students. And isn't that what all dedicated teachers strive for?

Let's Play Ball

There is no denying that we lived in a male chauvinist era; that mind set permeated all aspects of our lives. The women in this timber region additionally had the deck stacked against them inasmuch as they lived with and amongst the worst of the worst. Not that the men were mean or abusive. Oh, sure, there were some. It was that, by general acclamation, they ruled the roost.

But the one outstanding exception to this rule was our school's athletic program. No gender discrimination existed here; girls' athletics were well-funded, enthusiastically coached, and as strongly supported as the boys'.

Because of our small size, we fell into the classification of a "B" school. The girls' sports program included both a softball and volleyball team, which competed against other schools within our class. The same as the boys, the girls on the teams were expected to attend after-school practice. Added to that, as part of the curriculum each day, we attacked rigorous gym classes. Few excuses were acceptable for the avoidance of either.

The worthy opponents we played came from schools in places with such names as Yoncalla, Drain, Elkton, Glide, Glendale, Myrtle Creek, Camas Valley and Coos River. Anywhere from 20 to 80 miles away in any direction, we loaded onto the school bus for these out-of-town trips. The driver had to be on his toes as he herded the bus over the crooked, narrow two-lane roads that coiled around the mountains separating the towns.

During the winter, the girls' volleyball team accompanied the boys' basketball team. In the spring the girls' softball and the boys' baseball teams traveled together.

Participation in these sports became a high priority for many of us. For a few of the boys, it probably stood out as the chief reason they remained in school. For me, I loved it. So much so that my love-life ran a close second. But, having the best of both worlds, put the icing on the cake. These games offered a larger and more varied inventory of the opposite sex from which to shop.

It goes without saying that most of the players' parents showed up to boost our athletic events. And the enthusiastic general public turnout, per ratio, would put larger cities to shame. All to their credit, the girls' teams boasted as loyal a following and cheering section as did the boys'.

There She Goes

To say that the addition of Jo Ann Amorde to the teaching staff somewhat increased the male attendance at our softball games would be an understatement. A gorgeous, statuesque, 20-year-old, blue-eyed blond, she was hired to teach girls' P.E. and coach girls' athletics.

It was March, 1947 when Jo Ann signed an emergency contract to replace either a retiring or fatigued retreating teacher. Already into our spring softball/baseball season, Jo Ann took over coaching the girl's softball team. No one could have foreseen, that come summer, she would hurl Sutherlin into the limelight and put us on the map.

Jo Ann was a dazzler. Blessed with a captivating smile, and a figure to match, she paced the sidelines in her white shorts while animatedly urging us on. This energetic coaching couldn't help but draw attention away from who was on first and who was on second.

After only a few days on the job, she removed me from my chosen, somewhat safe position at second base. To my dismay, she stuck me in the more direct line of fire as shortstop between first and second. Why she moved me, I never knew, but I detested that position.

I much preferred second base because fewer balls chanced to be hit in that direction, and, therefore, fewer chances popped up to miss a zinging grounder and look stupid. Then too, I could hope that the pitcher, standing directly up in front of me, would run interference and catch the ball first. Standing on or near second base, looking all confident, poised, and in control, my demeanor implied, "I'd have caught that if she hadn't jumped at it first."

The girls' teams didn't have a lot of heavy hitters, and a good share of the balls came bounding, flying, or erratically bouncing along the ground towards shortstop. The probability of someone else getting to the ball first was less likely. I reasoned, if you want to look good, don't put yourself in a position where you might look bad!

Of course, when you effortlessly caught a flyball in your glove, or gracefully snatched it off the ground and, with a straight-as-an-arrow aim, fired it to first putting the runner out, you felt on top of the world. But when you awkwardly fumbled the ball or threw it over the head of the first baseman (on a really bad day the potential existed to do both), and the grinning runner now stood safe on second, you felt like the lowest of the low.

At that moment, I wished that whatever alien beings propelled the silver disks just beginning to be spotted flashing through the skies, would choose me to whisk away. I'd have willingly sacrificed myself to the God of Errors and Omissions for useless experimental purposes, thereby disappearing from the face of the earth forever.

✷   ✷   ✷

The Amorde family lived in the Douglas County Housing Project west of town, one of the housing projects hastily thrown up at the height of the war. Although lacking in superfluous amenities, it was home to 100 families. Were it not for this project, Sutherlin would have become a tent city. In addition to Jo Ann's involvement in girls' athletics, her contract called for her to teach music and science. Whatever class she stood in front of, she managed to hold the dazzled boys' undivided attention.

In the summer of 1947, at the urging of family and friends, Jo Ann entered the Miss Roseburg Contest and walked away with the title.

Culminating her entry into further competition in Portland, she was ceremoniously crowned Miss Oregon. She instantly became the pride of Sutherlin. Jo Ann held the distinction of being Oregon's first-ever entry in the Miss American Pageant in Atlantic City where she placed in the semi-finals. Understandably, she declined to teach the next year, and instead headed for Portland to accept a job offer in the fashion industry.

One good turn deserves another. The following season, our girls' softball team did the town and Jo Ann proud by winning Douglas County's Northern Division Girls' Softball Championship. Now, this might not sound like much to make a fuss about to more cosmopolitan folks, but considering that Douglas County is one of the largest in the nation, for our little burg it was downright exciting.

✳   ✳   ✳

All in all, we were blessed with dedicated teachers—some great and some mediocre. We took advantage of the education offered, and its importance was hammered into us. Those students having family funds available to pursue higher education found no difficulty in being accepted into the college of their choice.

No community junior colleges existed to afford us a second chance, or which we could use as a stepping stone to a four-year college. You either had it together by graduation, or else you could forget it. The exception to this barrier were the Korean War veterans. By way of the G.I. Bill, any number of these young men jumped at a second opportunity to further their education and chalked up fortunate outcomes.

Scant encouragement was given for young girls to go on to college, and if they did, the primary goal was to land a young man with prospects for a bright future.

The boys felt the tug of the ever-present temptation to leave school for the readily available jobs and abundant dollars awaiting them in the logging industry. Yet, most stuck to their guns and, with heads held high, walked across the stage to receive their diplomas.

We knew the rules and conformed, more often than not without complaining. The thought that rules should be changed to accommodate us, either individually or as a group, never crossed our minds. We didn't protest, and we made no demands. We were a compliant generation.

We were patriotic and proud of our country.

Born into the nucleus of our parents' fight for survival during the Depression, we witnessed and lived with their day-to-day struggles and hardships. It made a deep imprint on our subconscious.

Money was scarce for the majority of our families. Many of us held part-time jobs to either defray our own expenses or to add to the family's meager budget.

Taking nothing for granted, a real concern lurked in our minds about our future. A job was to be prized. We knew all too well that any wrong decisions we made, we lived with. We were raised to accept the consequences of our actions and expected no quarter of anyone. That life wasn't fair was a given.

We didn't have it all, but in so many ways we had it better.

CHAPTER FOUR

Of Cherry Cokes, Penicillin, and Bawdy Houses

As do most teenagers, I longed for the day when I'd be out of my parents' line of view. I looked forward to graduation, and promised myself I'd land a job that provided me with more than pocket change.

At home we barely made do, but managed to keep the wolf at bay. Still, my circumstances were little different from most of my schoolmates. Lacking a Big Brother governmental agency to enlighten us as to our underprivileged status, we exemplified the expression "ignorance is bliss." Enterprising and down-to-earth, we latched on to and took advantage of any hand up offered, never expecting a hand out.

For my part, despite Oregon's winter rains and gloomy days, life was good and each day was filled with adventure.

From my limited experience and brief glimpses into the behind-the-scenes goings-on of the townsfolk, I understood that the adult world could be cold and dreary. On the other hand, it held a garden of delights from which I was eager to harvest a bushel of fruit.

During my last two years of high school I began testing the waters that trickled towards my independence, all the while hoping my parents wore their blinders.

The greatest part of my afterschool hours were spent in town divided between the Nicolazzi and Grabow households. This allowed for easy-access, prearranged double dates and after-hours school activities—any excuse to remain in town and away from the isolation and work at home.

For lack of any special event, we hung out at the Sweet Shoppe, the local teenage gathering place. Here the menu offered everything any good soda fountain should: grilled cheese sandwiches, hamburgers, hot fudge sundaes, root beer floats, cherry Cokes or cherry phosphates, and thick milk shakes whipped in stainless steel shakers that filled two standard-size glasses.

The Rand Theatre, the local movie house, awaited movie-goers several doors down the street. Open every night, the management advertised three new features a week. As long as the money held out, we were committed to catch every change of movie; this held true for many of the adults as well. It was unusual to miss a war movie, western, or current Debbie Reynolds' musical.

After all, if you missed a featured show, you might find yourself on the outside looking in the next time you showed up for work or school. The magic that flickered across the screen would be savored and mulled over by the movie-goers until the next change of show. Other diversions were few and far between.

Bouts of anxiety jumped up and grabbed us girls if we failed to nail down a date for the latest show. But feigning a lack of concern, we managed to find our own way there and pay our own way in.

Although forced to attend a flick unaccompanied, we stood a good chance of catching a ride home. "Going Dutch" was uncommon, and the price of two tickets, plus the obligatory popcorn, was out of reach for many of the high school boys. But they were resourceful. Assured of finding girls looking for a way home other than hoofing it, they killed time by driving around aimlessly until the show let out. We managed to run into each other within the limited range of the town's two main blocks.

The Doctor Is In

Until the end of my Junior year, for the most part my after-school hours were spent at Dr. Grabow's house.

Prior to Doctor Grabow's arrival with his family in 1946, the town had been without a doctor for some time. Anyone needing routine medical attention made the drive to Roseburg, also the location of the nearest hospital.

Leaving Oakland, California, after war's end and his stint in both the U.S. Army and Navy, Dr. Grabow came to Sutherlin to take his place as the town's sole dispenser of medical advice and treatment. Besides general medical care and delivering babies, which predictably peaked in late summer—the result of the long wet winters—he found much of his practice taken up with treating the numerous injuries that occurred all too often in the woods and sawmills.

Prior to making the move to Sutherlin, the Grabows purchased a large, white two-story house on the western edge of town, along with a small amount of acreage. It was an unpretentious house, yet fitting of their position. The house occupied a knoll surrounded by a small grove of fir trees and overlooked the bottom acreage. Their land ended at Comstock Road.

A long graveled driveway afforded access to the Grabow residence, which driveway ended at a small porch on the south side of the house. This porch provided entry into the kitchen and was the everyday entrance. Off to the right of the house set a large carport constructed to house their two Cadillacs, with a third stall for any additional vehicle.

Shortly after arriving at school at the beginning of my Sophomore year, Bebe Grabow, the oldest daughter, and I became inseparable friends. Not being a whirlwind of activity, my home became mainly a place from which to depart—that is, when I could pull it off. Despite the Grabows having four children, and another on the way, their house became my home away from home, and they treated me as a welcome family member.

By reason of her birth order, the duties of chief babysitter for the younger children fell upon Bebe. Unwittingly, this laid the groundwork for my draft as assistant.

More often than not, this babysitting scenario amounted to a lot of, "I'm going to tell," blurted out by either the keepers or the keepees. Having little occasion to be around babies or young children, I found them nothing less than a source of extreme aggravation. I took part merely as a detached observer and morale booster.

Compared to my much older and inhibited parents, Dr. and Mrs. Grabow were both in their late thirties and openly displayed an abundance of affection toward each other. I relished the time spent at their home. It was a far cry from what I considered to be the tomb-like quiet of my house.

Barbara Grabow, a graduate of Smith's College, stood out as an extremely attractive, dark-complexioned woman with shiny attractively styled black hair. Her striking ebony eyes sparkled and snapped with life when she talked.

Dr. Grabow's face was set off by a rather square jaw line and heavy jowls. His husky build overwhelmed his height giving him the appearance of being of average height, although taller. Both inside and outside the office he displayed an indefatigable zest for life, and despite his demanding practice, gravitated towards and vigorously sought out other challenges. After squeezing in time for flying lessons at Sutherlin's new postage stamp-sized airport, he acquired his pilot's license. The purchase of a small fourseater airplane followed.

Whenever the weather permitted and his hectic practice allowed, he hopped in his plane and took off for Portland in search of a little rest and relaxation. Not too keen on air flight, Mrs. Grabow set down a firm rule that allowed only two children to accompany him on these flights. She loaded the other children in the Cadillac for a more leisurely cruise to Portland.

Secretly Salivating Over Salem

After being invited along on one of these flights up north, and gaining my folks' okay, I jumped at the chance. At that time, few opportunities arose for everyday folks to zoom off into the wild blue yonder.

DOC'S NEW AIRPLANE, 1949.
Doctor and Mrs. Grabow,
Judy and Jake in the new airplane.

When the big day came, Doc took his place at the controls and Bebe occupied the front passenger seat. With me securely buckled into one of the back seats, we taxied out on Sutherlin's meager airstrip and were soon airborne. The drone of the plane made audible conversation difficult, so I set back and took in the view from the small window.

But 45 minutes or so out, the desire for chitchat gave way to the necessity of swallowing a sudden unexpected overflow of saliva. The sickening queasy feeling in the pit of my stomach became the center of my attention. I did my best to hide my airsickness, figuring I could tough it out to Portland, with no one the wiser.

Without warning, Doc tipped the wings of the small bobbing plane and motioned off to the left cheerfully exclaiming, "There's Salem. About another 20 minutes we'll be landing in Portland."

That sudden wobbly maneuver did it. Beads of perspiration began oozing from my clammy forehead, and I knew my next attempted swallow was doomed to fail. Whitefaced and leaning over the front seat, I whispered to Bebe, "You'd better give me the brown bag."

At that moment, I devoted a brief prayer for divine intervention in the form of engine trouble culminating in an emergency landing. I'd have welcomed even a minor non-injury crash landing—at least I'd be on the ground. On the return trip home, without a spark of protest, I joined the ranks of Mrs. Grabow's grounded passengers and begged off any further invitations to ride the skies.

House Calls and the Debut of Penicillin

The Grabow household surged with activity from early morning until after sundown. With few exceptions, every evening after dinner Dr. Grabow grabbed his black bag loaded with medicinal paraphernalia and dashed off in his Caddie to make house calls. On occasion Mrs. Grabow accompanied Doc on his rounds, leaving Bebe and me unwillingly in charge of the dishes and the younger children. This

afforded them the opportunity to snatch a few moments to themselves and a chance to mull over the day's events.

On those rare occasions when he was allowed to enjoy an entire evening at home, the ringing phone—foretelling some emergency or a presumptive one—interrupted the respite.

Having developed quite a reassuring bedside manner of her own, Mrs. Grabow adeptly handled many of the phone calls while Dr. Grabow made his house calls. Often the worried caller's mind was put to rest by the mere sound of her confident voice on the other end of the line prescribing a bit of common sense.

Over time, for cases of "new mother's nerves," she became proficient at deciphering what the bumpy rash might typify and dispensing advice as to how best to take a temperature or calm a crying baby. Weeding out the more serious complaints requiring medical attention, she assured the caller that, upon his return home, Doc would call them back.

On more than one occasion I witnessed a dinner interrupted by an urgent knock on the door. Answering the summons at the side porch, Dr. Grabow could about anticipate what he'd find when he swung open the screen door. As often as not, there stood a disheveled fidgety logger shuffling from one foot to the other and grimacing from pain. Or, motioning towards the idling car where his bruised buddy sat slumped in the front seat, rushing to explain the situation.

Just as likely awaiting his response, he'd be greeted by an anxious father. After identifying himself and apologizing for bothering him at home, he'd explain that he didn't have a phone; then blurt out his concern about his sick child's skyrocketing temperature. Or, answering the door, he'd encounter a frantic mother with a feverish, wheezing child in tow.

Whatever the case, if needed, Doctor Grabow made arrangements to meet them down at his office to stitch up a laceration, apply a splint to an injured limb, or minister to a sick child.

As was often the case, the emergency might just as easily be handled under the dim glow of the porch light. Should an angry wound show signs of infection, or if a high fever and chest congestion warranted it, a shot of penicillin—the first of the antibiotics and the new wonder drug—might be just what the doctor ordered. Excusing himself, he'd hurry back inside the kitchen, snatch his doctor's bag off the end of the counter, and dash back to his patient. Out of the family's view, a hurried drop of the poor sufferer's pants, and a shot of penicillin injected into a bare cheek, now rudely exposed to the nippy night air, handled the matter. At least for the present. Next came follow-up instructions to drop by the office next day.

The most common grumbling of the townspeople regarding Doc Grabow's treatment was, "He always tells you 'take two aspirins and call me in the mornin'.'" Then stumbling or limping into the office the next day, no matter what the hell's wrong with you, you get a damned penicillin shot."

In all fairness, were it not for many of those perceived overprescribed penicillin shots, the tally of the all-too-frequent logging deaths and loss of limbs would have been greater. The community already experienced an unnerving number each year. For every ineffectual shot administered, two effectively prevented a festering leg injury from winding up as an amputation, or a harsh cough from turning into pneumonia, or a diagnosed case of pneumonia ending in death.

✻   ✻   ✻

Dr. Grabow, bound by the usual professional ethics, kept to himself the populace's infirmities and medical problems. Although assured of her trustworthiness, I'm sure on occasion he shared certain noteworthy medical matters with Mrs. Grabow. Nevertheless, by purposely overhearing an off-handed hushed conversation or a dropped remark, Bebe and I glommed onto what run-of-the-mill illnesses were going around. Grimacing, we took in the gory details of yesterday's logging accident. We were all ears when her Dad made note of the latest case of syphilis miraculously responding to penicillin. (Word of this was slyly dropped for our benefit to reinforce the dangers of sex.)

Penicillin, which attacked a myriad of infections and infectious diseases, proved its true potential during WWII. It became the first humane treatment for syphilis. This disease hit its share of folks in this wide-open logging town. Earlier syphilis treatment required a hospital setting with painful intravenous infusions of a mercury/arsenic combination; thus the old English sailors' lament, "One night with Venus, six months with Mercury."

Sulfa drugs used in the 1930s for the treatment of the other dreaded venereal disease, gonorrhea, most times proved ineffectual. Penicillin became the primary treatment for this affliction.

Bawdy Houses

One evening, unable to any longer keep the salacious news to herself, and after swearing me to secrecy for the fifth consecutive time, Bebe confided, "There's going to be a new whorehouse over by the football field, and Daddy's going to take care of the girls!"

Now this jerked me to attention. I wrangled from her all the juicy privileged scuttlebutt she knew, beginning with, "What did 'taking care of the girls' mean'?"

This spicy tidbit afforded us numerous giggles and fueled the vehicle of our whirling imaginations to run amuck.

Unlike the seasonal slumps affecting other businesses in town, this upstart enterprise couldn't help but thrive since it wouldn't have to battle those odds. Ideally located one block south of our school athletic field, it was perfect for walk-in business. It sat tucked away on a street near the old Chenoweth home.

The Chenoweths were a longtime, established family in the area, and as is common in small towns, certain older homes function as identifying points of reference. One of a row of finer houses, their two-story fronted the road paralleling the football/baseball playing field, now the site of the City Park.

The Sutherlin Creek, meandering a distance behind this new pleasure palace, served to protect the backside of the house, all the while the frontside was shielded by certain of the city fathers.

The powers-that-be knew full well that when the city's chief of police, whom we shall call Bob Bingham, didn't have his head stuck in the sand, it was conveniently turned the other way. Then suddenly he vaporized overnight, coincidentally about the same evening as a planned raid by the State Police.

His hasty departure set the wheels of the rumormill to spinning. One circulating theory for his hitting the bricks was that he'd been fired by the Mayor because of his well-known affair with a local businessman's warm-hearted wife. The other gossip making the rounds: that the chief and one of the town's enterprising real estate men were in cahoots as proprietors of the fledgling brothel.

Neither of these presumptions surprised the inner-circle of knowledgeable townsfolk, and in reality either flying rumor stood a good chance of being true. In any event, unable to weather the storm, the "hurriedly departed" popped up on the police force in another small town somewhere in Eastern Oregon.

Several years later the report came down that Bob was killed in the line of duty. As word spread, this became the topic of the day. The story read that he happened upon a burglary in progress and in attempting to arrest the burglar he was confronted with a gun. In the tussle to wrest the gun away, it went off leaving Bob mortally wounded. After the initial shock of his death wore off, those unwilling to let the poor fellow die a brave and meritorious death rethought the scenario. They believed it more likely that the weapon he struggled to seize was clutched in the hands of another irate cuckold husband.

✳ ✳ ✳

Ruth's El Rancho, an established competitor to the latest house of ill repute, sat unobtrusively atop a knoll back off Highway 99. Surrounded and screened by a fortress of oaks, it was ideally almost centrally located between Sutherlin and Roseburg. Being about six miles from Sutherlin gave the town an edge over Roseburg by several miles.

There could be no doubt that this new venture would divert some business away from Ruth's. It stood to reason that those Sutherlin gentlemen momentarily preoccupied by the fit of their skivvies would head for the closest wenching sanctuary.

There wasn't a time I passed by that hill, either driving or riding as a passenger, whether going to or coming from Roseburg, that I didn't feel compelled to cast a quick glance up to the green house. Not that I made a comment to anyone. I'm not sure what I expected to catch sight of, but I'd have settled for anything of a suspicious nature as proper payoff for my constant surveillance.

One telltale sign I kept a lookout for was the proverbial red light. Despite having good eyes, I couldn't spot one, and concluded it must be out of sight somewhere towards the back. How could anyone find the place if the ladies didn't advertise?

I was too naive to realize that this place operated on a need-to-know basis only. And those who needed to know already knew!

It struck me odd during those years and hundreds of trips past the hill, that not once did I see a car pulled up in front. Nor did I ever see any outward sign of either normal or suspicious activity. The house appeared entirely unoccupied except for glowing lights visible at night. Frustrated by my inability to spot any shady goings-on, I began to question whether it was really what it was reputed to be, or another talltale that snowballed.

Having a brain not yet functional in deceit and deviousness, I failed to realize that discretion dictated that parking be reserved at the back of the house where trees hid everything from view.

At any rate, logic, of which I was in short supply, should have told me that customers wouldn't arrive at the house in the same manner as the Fuller Brush Man or the Avon Lady. They didn't pull up to the front of the house, park, then saunter up to the front door and knock.

Taking all my mediocre, nonsensical facts to their opposite logical conclusion, the complete lack of any sign of activity whatsoever during all that time, except the lights at night, should have been a clue. An astute, suspicious person would have picked up on the fact that this was not your normal, everyday sort of household operating up there; nor was anyone heavy into gardening or growing beefsteak tomatoes.

* * *

Anyway, besides the white two-story house near the Union Service Station fronting on Highway 99, Ruth's was due further competition. Keeping this confidence presented no problem, as I'd heard about Ruth's El Rancho for such a long time that I presumed it to be common knowledge.

I reasoned that Dr. Grabow's desire to keep his new patients secret was because this knowledge might offend the sensibilities of certain of his genteel patients—at least those not anticipating getting in on the action.

One day as Bebe and I strolled along on the opposite side of the street from Doc's office, I received a vicious jab in the ribs from her bony elbow.

Cupping a hand over the far side of her mouth, she whispered, "Quick, quick, look! But, don't really look! Pretend not to look. What I mean is, don't let them see you look! Two of the prostitutes I told you about are walking into Daddy's office."

"How in the hell can I look, if I can't look?"

"Just look sideways, but don't let them see you!"

Glancing out of the side of my eyes, I took in all I could, and my first reaction was extreme disappointment. In all the Westerns I'd sat through, the prostitutes or dance hall girls stood out in glittery, seductive finery and overdone makeup.

They always wore beautiful fancy gowns with a feather or some form of adornment coyly tucked into their ravishingly beautiful hair. Their plentiful bosoms bulged out of and flowed over the top of their gorgeous lowcut dresses.

Indeed, not that I'd given it a lot of serious thought, but that profession was one of the first I'd ruled out for myself as even a slight possibility should all else fail.

I didn't stand a snow ball's chance in hell of passing muster, mainly because of the lowcut dress bit. Disadvantaged, I'd have a damn hard time making my bosom spill out over the top of anything, even with a little help from a few folded handkerchiefs.

In my musings about these heretofore imaginary women, I believed an intense, mysterious aura of intrigue would emanate from and hover about them—something so overpowering and seductive that you could sense it. Just some shadowy sign indicating that they lived in a sleazy, quivering quagmire of wickedness and sin would have satisfied me.

Obviously, something was lost in the translation from my mind to reality. Here were two deceptively normal, average-looking, everyday sort of women completely devoid of glamour or elegance. They didn't fit the picture of brassy painted ladies and withheld any flaunting of cleavage. This was strictly nofrills packaging.

Right after that sorry incident, I kind of lost interest.

Shipped Off

Prior to our Senior year at Sutherlin High, Bebe was hustled off to a girl's school in Seattle in preparation for entry into the University of Washington. There were several reasons for this maneuver besides the obvious one of obtaining a good solid education. Going along with the thought of the day, this move would serve as her passport to meet Mr. Right and marry well, thereby warding off Doc's worst fear that she'd end up with a goddamned logger!

Not that this was a misguided decision. For the most part, tying up with a logger meant coming to grips with living a life of full-blown insecurity—emotional as well as financial. By and large, it was a hand-to-mouth existence. For every entrepreneurial logger who beat the odds and prospered, 50 went belly-up.

And despite their image as unkempt, hard-drinking, itinerant rascals—which held true for a certain percentage—those who settled down, married, and fathered children, as often as not took on the role of devoted family men and worked hard to provide for their families.

Insurance statistics spoke for themselves and confirmed what the timber industry already knew that occupation-wise, logging fell under jobs classification as being the most hazardous.

A logger's wife took in stride the reality that one day the family's sole breadwinner could suffer a devastating crippling injury, leaving him temporarily disabled at best and permanently disabled at worst.

Each morning that he trudged off to work she did her best to shove aside the foreboding that wrapped around her like a dark flannel robe—that this could very well be the day his time ran out.

Having chosen this path, she shrugged her shoulders and learned to cope. She nipped these worries in the bud by relegating them to the furthest recesses of her mind. Yet, with each day's tally of casualties, the anxieties sprouted anew and shoved their way back into her thoughts.

By planning ahead and whisking his oldest daughter out of town before any serious involvement, Doc Grabow got his wish. Bebe didn't end up with a logger!

PART TWO

PAUL BUNYON:

WHERE'S YOUR OX?

GLOSSARY

Logging Terms

The non-technical, brief, and succinct terms and descriptions in this glossary are written for the layman. They specifically refer to the timber harvesting practices as performed in the Douglas fir region of Oregon during the 1940s and 1950s. It is understood that despite the evolution of newer and safer techniques in harvesting, they may still aptly apply to current methods and practices.

CAT SKINNER—The caterpillar (crawler tractor) operator who builds roads into the woods, skids cut logs to the *landing*, and levels the selected spot for the landing.

CHOKER SETTER—Sets cable choker (lengths of wire rope) around the end of the log. He then hooks it to the back of the tractor so it may be skidded or yarded into the *landing*. Considered an entry-level job in the woods.

CRUMMY—A panel wagon of old suburban (small bus) that was used to transport men back and forth from town to the woods.

FALLER AND BUCKER—A two-man team. One fells the tree with a chain saw, and the other uses his saw to trim and buck it (cut it up) into appropriate log lengths. Felling a large tree, they use a two-man power saw. Before the era of gas-powered saws, they each worked on one end of a cross-cut saw. In large timber operations, the two jobs may be performed by separate crews: a felling crew and a bucking crew.

GYPO (GYPPO)—A logger with a small operation employing a minimum of men. He also contracts out to larger operators to perform a portion or all of their logging.

LANDING—An area specifically selected relative to the surrounding terrain and the timber to be cut. This area is cleared of trees and brush and leveled by a bulldozer. The logs are then skidded or yarded to this spot for loading onto log trucks.

LOADING DONKEY—Also called a Skidding Donkey or Yarder. A gas or diesel-driven triple-drum winch that sits on a level spot some distance ahead of where the logging crew works. It winches logs out of steep canyons up to the landing for loading onto trucks. The donkey/yarder is used where the terrain is too steep to work a caterpillar. This also requires the use of a *spar pole*. This combination is called high-lead logging.

LOGGING SHOW—The actual area in the woods where the logging takes place.

SPAR POLE OR SPAR TREE—A tall, sturdy, straight and rooted tree that is first topped and secured with guywires (wire rope) to prevent it from snapping under the weight of logs being yarded in by the triple-drum *yarding donkey*. It is rigged with cables and blocks, which are used to pull the logs out of canyons and up the hillsides to the *landing*.

In early days, this was called a spar tree and could reach a height of as much as 200 feet.

In latter times, if tree the correct size (average 90 to 100 feet) couldn't be found for this purpose, a fallen tree was skidded to to the landing site, raised, secured, and rigged. This is termed a spar pole.

TOPPER OR HIGH CLIMBER—A logger who rigs spar trees or poles. He is equipped with long, spiked-climbing spurs strapped to his boots and legs and wears a special belt with a steel-core climbing rope attached. This belt is extra wide and extra strong and has dangling from it a razor-sharp ax and saw. He wraps the steel-cored climbing rope around the tree, securing himself to it.

As he begins his ascent, he flips the rope eight to ten feet ahead of himself upward on the tree then hitches himself aloft. Along the way he lops off the limbs with the ax or the saw.

Twenty to thirty feet before reaching the top, or at a point where the tree's diameter is about 24 inches, he digs in his spurs and secures himself to the tree with the loosely-looped rope. Then, with the ax and saw he cuts the top out of the tree. He attaches a small block to the top of the spar and threads a passline through it. This will be used to pull up the blocks and guylines needed to complete the rigging.

WIDOW-MAKER—A heavy limb loosely dangling or lodged in a tree, ready to fall should it be disturbed or limbs or snags that snap off a carelessly felled tree or one that mistakenly crashes into standing timber.

Also, often categorized as such is any debris lying on the forest floor that may have become dislodged and airborne at the instant a tree slammed to the ground. These objects have the potential to become deadly missiles, catapulting in any or many directions through the air with as much deadly force as a rifle shot.

If at any moment you are within line of one of these falling limbs, hurtling limbs, or other debris—your wife in all probability is now a widow.

CHAPTER FIVE

No Place to Hide: The Forested Homefront
Pre-War Inland Logging

Encompassing over 5,000 square miles, the vast timberlands in Douglas County remained virtually untouched prior to the 1940s. Here stood the greatest and finest stand of virgin Douglas fir in the state. Within the county's boundaries awaiting the timber cutters' saws was the largest volume of saw timber in any single county in the United States.

Whatever inland timber cutting the early settlers engaged in was insignificant. Their primary purpose in chopping down trees was to ready the land for sheep and cattle grazing. They utilized these downed trees for firewood or milled whatever they needed for their own purposes. Later on, as more inland mills sprung up, their customer base remained mainly the settlers themselves.

In 1925, the first year the Oregon Department of Forestry began keeping timber harvest records, 23 steam-powered sawmills were recorded in Douglas County. In 1932, in the midst of the Depression, that number decreased to a low of 18. The majority of these were small family-operated mills that only ran intermittently and their production was minuscule. This timber cutting failed to make a dent in what then appeared to be the county's inexhaustible forests.

It wasn't until the late 1920s that tractors and trucks came on the scene for use in the Douglas fir region to increase timber harvesting and facilitate the transportation of logs to mill sites.

Torching the Timber

Right up until the beginning of WWII, many of the ranchers in Douglas County held the view that the timber on their forested mountains was useless for anything much except firewood. They considered their land's value not to be in the number of board feet of timber, but once they could rid themselves of the pesky trees, in the amount of acreage available for pasture.

On these mountainsides stood giant towering trees so thick that sunlight, essential for growing grass, was unable to penetrate. As their sheep and cattle herds grew and more grazing land was needed, the timber on these mountains was cut, and the downed trees and underbrush burned.

Nancy Nichols Gallop's great-grandparents were early pioneers who traveled the old Oregon Trail. The family finally settled in Brockway, west of Roseburg. As a child in the late 1930s, Nancy recalls accompanying her mother to watch the burning of an entire mountain of virgin timber. Hundreds and hundreds of trees in this dense green belt were set on fire to make way for needed pasture. Her family referred to this grassland as the "mountain pasture," and at the beginning of each summer their sheep were moved there to graze.

The Baimbridge family who settled and ranched in and around the Oakland area owned 1400 acres of land, much of which was forested. Like elsewhere in the county, these dense forests were impenetrable by the rays of the midday sun, and semidarkness prevailed.

Using axes and crosscut saws, they also "slashed" their timber and burned it. But being frugal and pennywise, they first cut the Douglas fir into firewood, which supplied their customers in the community with winter wood. Then the downed timber, including mammoth trees found too difficult to split, was sent up in flames.

It was backbreaking work, but they were ranchers and their livelihood depended on pasture for their growing herds of livestock. The damned infernal trees with the tangle of ferns and underbrush had to go!

Although they prospered, within a decade many of these same ranchers, shocked at the price timber was going for, were exclaiming, "Oh, my God, what did I do?"

Changing Viewpoint and Landscape

Nine months after the beginning of World War II, the September 25, 1942, *Sutherlin Sun* heralded the opening of the Smith Woods Camp, a logging camp 18 miles east of Sutherlin near the Calapooya River. The camp was to provide homes for 125 workmen and employ twelve trucks. All cut timber would be transported into Sutherlin Timber Products, one of the larger mills in town. Looking forward, the company announced the acquisition of its own rock crusher, thereby affording them the convenience of crushing rocks at the logging site. This enabled them, with minimal expense, to gravel their logging roads, making them passable during the rainy winters. The front page announcement read:

> On a hundred hills, from a hundred slopes in Sutherlin vicinity comes the woodcutters' cry. Two axmen run as they shout the warning: a forest plant snaps its last supporting sinews, moves with majestic grace as the topmost branches soar through the sky, gather momentum quickly and fall with a swelling roar and crash. One hundred feet of straight timber. All the years since Columbus are recorded in the concentric rings in its log of life. A great historian is dead But the life of service has just begun. The government will have more ships, more airplanes and more pontons [pontoons], and families can have more homes…

The government continued to hound the logging industry for more and more lumber for the war effort. Ironically, that war of itself caused critical shortages of the very materials needed to produce this coveted lumber. The May 1, 1942, *Sutherlin Sun's* headlines, "Critical Need for Log Truck Tires," depicted the seriousness of the situation. It reported that there were no tires for log trucks; that 90% of all sawmill production in the state was on war orders, and a large part of those orders were due to be halted within three months unless tires for trucks were provided. The story went on:

> . . . citing the situation in Douglas County, where all log hauling is done by trucks, [U.S. Representative] Ellsworth said that the requirement is 250 tires monthly, but that the quota has been only 55-60. The Rationing Board had only four tires left in the April quota with 25 applications [still] on file.

Because of this immediate need for lumber, the opportunity for loggers and far-sighted entrepreneurs created the climate for the logging boom. They rushed to set up small mills to process these logs; this was to provide the avenue for many of the fortunes made in the timber industry.

A Common Man Achieving Uncommon Things

The seeds for one of those fortunes were already in the ground prior to Smith Woods arrival on the scene and prior to the War.

In 1936, at the age of 28, Kenneth Ford built his first sawmill out of salvaged and scavenged equipment. He named it Roseburg Lumber Co. This mill was just east of Roseburg and employed 25 people.

These were not easy years for the Fords, and despite the Depression, they hung on. Through it all, Ford always paid his employees before he paid himself, and most of his profits went back into the business.

Towards the end of 1939, because of an inadequate log supply brought on by bad weather, Kenneth Ford decided to begin logging a tract of timber he had earlier purchased 16 miles east of Sutherlin at Hinkle Creek.

Ford, working along side his men, built two bridges and a mile of plank road so they could get the logs rolling to the mill six or eight weeks sooner than normal. Before this undertaking, Ford informed the men that he could only pay them $1.00 a day, but he would fare no better and would eat the same bean diet on which they subsisted.

He is fondly remembered by his early employees as a man who wouldn't ask them to do anything he wouldn't do. Work was his pleasure; he thought nothing of putting in an 18-hour day. His philosophy was, "There's no elevator to success; you have to take the stairs."

One of his early Sutherlin employees, John Bratton, worked for him "right in the camp" during those early years. He described the camp

---

BOOM
(*Top*) The boom lifted logs up to weigh it.

OLD RD8 PAINTED ARMY GREEN
(*Bottom*) Ford was unable to get parts for his old equipment and was tickled to purchase this cheap from the U.S. Army.

as having a bunk house, a cook shack and an office. As money would allow, these were all upgraded and bare-bone housing built.

After asking John Bratton about Kenneth Ford, the first words out of his mouth were, "He was one great man to start out like he did!" The enthusiasm in his voice reflected his great respect and admiration for Mr. Ford.

John said he left Mr. Ford to go logging for himself, and Mr. Ford gave him the timber. I inquired, "You mean you paid him a set price for what you cut?"

"No," he replied. "He GAVE it to me! And, he built me a house in Sutherlin."

After inquiring if Ford had done this by way of appreciation for John's standing by him in the lean years, John stated that he didn't think so, he just did it for him. And he did other things to help him. "He was just that kind of a man."

✳   ✳   ✳

The opening of a large logging operation such as the one at Smith Woods Camp was the impetus that brought more loggers (and the greenhorns anticipating work) to the region. The additional perk of housing at the logging site gave the larger operator a distinct advantage over the small-scale gypos. They could more readily attract and hire hard-to-find workers. Whether the deferments given to "men performing essential tasks in lumber camps, mills and mines" contributed to the men's attraction to the woods and mills can only be surmised.

During the years spanning the War, the timber workers could never work fast enough to keep up with the demand.

SCALE
(*Right*) Scale secured to tree to weigh log.

BUNKHOUSE, EARLY 1940s
(*Bottom*) Bunkhouse from Ford's Camp at Mt. Scott. Photograph courtesy of Roseburg Forest Products

The Staggering Shopping List

Even before the United States was drawn into WWII, the British looked to us for lumber for aircraft. Forty-one types of British planes needed wooden parts for their Mosquito bombers and Hurricane fighters.

In the book *Head Rig*, a story of the West Coast lumber industry by Ellis Lucia, and in particular his chapter, "The Forests Go to War," a bright light is cast on the government's serious unrelenting dependency on lumber.

> "By the Spring of 1942, Colonel Greeley reported to the West Coast Lumbermen's Association members that there were war orders totaling 800,000,000 board feet at the mills..."

The Army alone needed three hundred trains of lumber, each train over a mile long. The demands were widespread and varied. There were the obvious needs for docks, wharves, cantonments, wagons, pontoons, bridges, ties, trench props and the like, everything from tent poles to the walls of boot camp obstacle courses. The government placed orders for 360 cargo ships, each requiring a sizable quantity of lumber. Even the big steel and iron battle wagons of the Navy needed upward to 500,000 board feet of lumber for decking and gun mounts; steel-hulled cargo ships required 700,000 board feet of lumber and 300,000 square feet of plywood. New-type training planes were being built of thin sheets of wood veneer.... Bombing planes packed for shipment by rail or water required about 15,000 board feet—the equivalent of lumber for a five-room house. The little hit-and-run mosquito boats needed 35,000 feet of Douglas fir, spruce, African mahogany and birch....By mid-1942 the projected needs of the War Production Board as to lumber were triple the 8,500,000,000 board feet estimated for a two-and-one-half year period a year earlier.

The government's shopping list went on and on, everything from wooden structures built with Douglas fir engineering to dummy cannons and planes to fool the enemy.

COOKHOUSE, EARLY 1940S
Cookhouse from Ford's Camp at Mt. Scott. Photograph courtesy of Roseburg Forest Products

In 1943 alone, 15 billion board feet of lumber were used to package (crating, boxing and dunnage) supplies, which included ammunition, needed by the military throughout the world.

Two years later, the ongoing shopping list proved insatiable: January 19, 1945 *Sutherlin Sun*

Paul Bunyan and Your Blue Ox, We Need Your Help—and Quick!
This is the appeal of the U.S. Army to the West Coast Logging and Lumber Industry. Lumber, most critical of all war materials, is most critically needed.

Every able-bodied logger on the job is the appeal. And from Major R. Chinn of the Army: 'Boys, we can't let up now. That's the appeal from every fighting man in Europe and on the Pacific. Give us boards, give us crated ammo, give us the lumber we need to finish this job. But be quick!'

Yet, Paul Bunyan's ox continued to be gored and hobbled by the shortages of essential materials.

Gearing Up

The start-up of a largescale logging operation in close proximity to a populated area was indeed a reason to rejoice; nevertheless, the major log suppliers were the independent gypos. These small logging operators were the steadfast backbone of the economy. The town lived on logging, either by way of working directly in the industry or secondarily, by providing services to those who did.

The gypo always kept an eye out for any small or, by his standards, large patch of timber to purchase and log. Once he found an interested prospective seller, he either "cruised" the timber himself or hired a cruiser. This job entailed walking the land, surveying the trees for quality, and estimating the number of board feet and value of merchantable timber in the region to be logged. Cruising was also essential to determine the land's topography, as the steepness of the slopes and the varying soil conditions determined the method of operation and how best to utilize his equipment. The operator then had the foresight to project road construction and harvesting costs.

Once the costs were estimated and allowance made for profit, he submitted his bid on the stumpage.

Next, a logging contract was drawn providing that as the timber was cut, the landowner would be paid based on the number of board feet removed. In order to operate with minimal men and equipment, the gypo's basic needs would be a cat/tractor, a loader, and a crummy. He might own a truck or two, but by and large he hired the independent gypo truckers to perform the hauling.

✳   ✳   ✳

After attending to the initial business-end of the details, including obtaining the obligatory rights-of-way, the gypo was ready to begin work. The first item on the agenda was the formidable task of "punching out" a passable road back into the timber to the spot chosen for the first landing. In the process of road building, he clears any rights-of-way acquired to afford access to his patch of timber.

Road building was accomplished by cutting any trees standing in the way, dynamiting or pushing out the remaining stumps with the bulldozer, and blading the road. If ditches were needed to divert water away from the roadbed, they must be excavated.

If by lucky happenstance a part of the land through which the road was to be built had already been logged, the logging operator could simply regrade whatever trace of road remained. Taking advantage of this saved many manhours.

Unlike today's landscape with its network of paved and graveled roads criss-crossing the countryside and winding around the remotest of mountains, 40 to 50 years ago the forests were more inaccessible.

Ordinarily, building a passable road into a virgin area was a major undertaking and highly labor-intensive. Those crude dirt logging roads could snake back into the wilderness as far as five or six miles off a graveled or paved main road.

For safety reasons, certain rules of the road applied to all vehicles traversing these primitive trails. It was understood that should two vehicles traveling in opposite directions meet, the uphill-bound vehicle must back down to a safe spot and pull off the road. Utilizing this turnout allowed the downward-bound vehicle to squeeze past. Like all rules, it had an exception, and that was the loaded log truck. Lacking the advantage of jockeying for position, it claimed the right of way. To facilitate this bypass, turnouts were created along the way wherever a convenient and adequate spot was found.

Fire in the Hole

In the course of building roads, the larger tree stumps that stood in the way and remained unfazed by the bulldozer's power were blown with dynamite. The object of this was not to blow the stump out of the ground, but merely to splinter or shatter it and to loosen and breakup the stump's roots. Now the bulldozer could push it out of the way with minimal effort.

As a rule, dynamiting was performed by "powder monkeys," who usually worked in pairs. This trade was learned via on-the-job training whereby one logger, successful enough to have survived, passed his knowledge on to another. In the larger companies, such as Weyerhaeuser, this was a single occupation performed by an experienced employee, and was the only role he filled. On the other hand, forever needing to cut corners, the economizing gypo used anyone already working for him in any capacity to perform the job. Should he allege a smidgen of training or a bit of knowledge, so much the better. After all, he hadn't killed himself or anyone else yet.

Even though you may enjoy it most days, what makes any job more pleasurable is the unanticipated humorous incident that provides a good hearty belly laugh and lifts everyone's spirits. It makes an otherwise longday short. A certain young logger friend, who hired on as a cat skinner on a small logging show, abruptly found himself commandeered as an "honorary" powder monkey.

Hobbled by a leg injury, the uneasy veteran logger explained to him, "You first dig the dirt out from around and under the stump's roots, just enough to shove a couple sticks of dynamite under it."

These sticks are then lit and blown, which results in a small cavity under the stump. Following this, a larger charge of dynamite is placed into this cavity and detonated, finally shattering and loosening the stubborn stump.

Explaining what to do next, the veteran departed the scene after short-sightedly telling the novice, "There's enough left in the box to blow it." Lost in this hasty instruction's translation was the meaning that, "there's more than enough…"

Hunkering down and attempting to act nonchalant, the novice nervously eyed the remaining dynamite sticks, then gingerly proceeded to load them into the dugout under the tree stump. As he'd been shown, he packed it with dirt and strung out the fuse. Having failed to reach an acceptable level of bravery at this new job, he made a long fuse.

Guided by his brief instructions, he touched a match to the fuse and yelled the obligatory "Fire in the Hole!"

With no time to lose, head down and teeth clenched, he took off on a dead run. His long legs afforded him the ability to cover the uneven terrain in long hurdling strides, while randomly performing a frantic tapdance over the littered slash and debris.

The thundering explosion that followed reverberated throughout the silence of the woods for miles around. And dirt, rocks, debris, and splinters rained down on the startled crew working near the landing more than a quarter mile away.

In the course of recounting his tale, he broke up with laughter and exclaimed, "the sky even turned black!" (No doubt the descending darkness could be attributable to the length of time it took to peep through scrunchedup eyes and observe the damage he wrought.) The yawning hole blown for this small stump, whose diameter he estimated to be five or six feet across, measured 30 feet across and 12 feet deep. For the next several days, pending scaring up enough dirt and debris to fill the newly created crater, further road building ceased. Since a thick stand of timber harbors little readily accessible dirt, finding fill-in material wasn't an easy task. What soil there is houses the invasive root systems of the giant trees and supports the growing abundance of thick vegetation beneath them.

No doubt this would be considered environmental blasphemy today. But 50 years ago, it was seen as merely a costly and inconvenient mishap that occurred while delivering the goods and accomplishing a job that needed to be done.

HIGH CLIMBER RIGGING SPAR TREE, 1960s
Photograph courtesy of the Douglas County Museum of History and Natural History.

The Logging Show

"Those guys don't know a damn thing!"

This was the abrupt response I received from a crusty old logging operator after saying, "You're one of the few old loggers around whose brain I can pick—the younger ones don't have the answers."

Rapid changes in technology and the introduction of newer models of equipment have rendered some of the old ways of logging obsolete. Yet, in many ways the basic practices and methods used in timber harvesting remain unchanged. For that reason, this portion of the chapter is written in present tense.

The Landing

After completion of road building, a landing is carved out of a selected area. The logging crew is set to begin work in earnest. If logging out of steep canyons where cats are unable to navigate, it is essential to locate this landing within the range of a tall tree sturdy enough to serve as a spar pole.

The landing is a temporary site. It is a cleared and leveled centrally located spot into which the felled and bucked logs are skidded for loading onto log trucks. It is situated relative to the timber to be logged. Once logging in that circumference is completed, the landing is moved to another selected site. Road is continually being punched out back into the timber, and those logs cut while road building are skidded back into the landing until its relocation. The road into the new landing is now either fully or partially forged.

It is much easier on men, equipment, and the environment to move the landing rather than skid massive logs a considerable distance through thick underbrush.

The Awesome Ways of Being Maimed

Fallers and buckers fell the timber, the choker setters rush to set the steel cable around the logs, then hook the cable onto the cat. The tension applied to the cable by the first tug of the cat serves to secure and set the chokers deep into the logs' course bark. The accelerating cat continues its crawl, laboring to pull the logs up to the landing—sometimes one at a time, sometimes two or more depending on their size.

Next, the man working as the loader sits astride the clattering loading machine stacking and arranging the logs by size onto the awaiting truck and trailer. For safe transport to the mills, the logs are secured in place by chains and binders tautly bound around the load.

During the course of each workday, the men face a mixture of hazards: the catapulting widow-makers, the razorsharp chains of the handheld power saws, the herding of log trucks up and down narrow and steeply inclined dirt roads, and the implicit dangers of working as a cat skinner.

Side Hill Style

Accepting these calculated risks is enough without the fear of the unforeseen surprise of slipping, stumbling, or falling while clambering over the myriad of debris, slash and slick fir needles. The chance of this happening is diminished by the wearing of steel-toed caulk boots, which the loggers call "corks." Not purporting to make you graceful and lightfooted, a pair of these boots weighs between six and seven pounds.

Exempted from wearing caulk boots is the cat skinner, who dons a regular work boot to run cat. The reason for this will be made evident.

All in all, there are no hard and fast rules about the wearing of specific work clothes in the woods. But common sense brings about a style that, at first glance, might appear a bit strange.

Fashion dictates butchering a brand-new pair of work pants by cutting off the first four inches of the legs. The main intent of this exercise is the elimination of the doubled-over and tightly sewn seam at the bottom of the leg. If an unaltered pant leg happens to get caught up in a twirling or twisting piece of machinery, that doubled-over seam could serve to make the pant leg act as a steel trap, pulling a man into the machinery's clutches. This practice also decreases the odds of having the pants' flapping cuffs (normally aligned with the bottom of the ankle) become ensnared on snags, limbs, underbrush, or any other visible or invisible menace, thereby causing a person to be thrown off balance.

While walking—perhaps encumbered with a razorsharp ax or a potentially impaling tool—should the bottom of a man's shorn pant leg, now adorned with short fringes, become entangled in moving machinery or ensnared on a snag, the pant leg can safely rip upward or tear away.

Whenever the fringes became a little too long, a quick touch of a flame from a match or cigarette lighter is all it takes to bring them back to an acceptable length.

MOBILE SPAR POLE AND LOADER
Used in place of a spar tree.
Photograph courtesy of Roseburg Timber Products.

The Fallers and Buckers: Which Way to Run?

The inherent quiet and tranquillity of the woods is challenged by the sound of buzzing power saws arduously grinding their way into the green virgin timber. These power saws are in the strong calloused hands of the fallers and buckers. Their job is to fell the trees and buck them to size.

Piloting a two-man gas-powered chain saw, sawdust flies and salty sweat bathes their faces, soaks their hickory shirts, and seeps into their thick broad suspenders as they labor on opposing sides of a large Douglas fir. Their mission: to severe it from the stump and bring it down. Larger, longer, and heavier than the one-man saw, this cutting implement may easily weigh 80 pounds and have a blade anywhere up to six feet long.

Positioned on opposite sides of the snarling chainsaw, one man controls the motor's speed. The other faller holds the stinger (handgrip) that positions the saw and applies the pressure needed for efficient cutting.

When working in smaller timber, each faller wields his own power saw, weighing anywhere between 35-50 pounds, and toils alone on a separate tree. For safety reasons they attempt to remain within sight of each other. The size and weight of the saws are dependent upon the size of the timber being cut. (It should be noted that today's chain saws weigh less and cut faster.)

After firing up the power saw, the selected tree is first undercut (notched at the tree's base) on the side facing the direction in which it is intended to fall. The depth of the undercut is determined by the tree's size.

Next, the heavy saw is lifted to near-waist height and turned at a right angle to begin its laborious cutting through the green, wet timber. Once the fast-cutting saw bites, it is not simply a matter of directing its journey into the tree's center, but for it to cut efficiently, a tremendous amount of pressure and force must be exerted.

LOGGER'S CAULK BOOTS

FALLER FALLING TREE ON DRAGON BACK MOUNTAIN
(*Top*) Near Riddle, Oregon, 1960s.
Photograph courtesy of the Douglas County
Museum of History and Natural History.

OLD AND NEW SAWS
(*Left*) Men holding two-man power saw.
Photograph courtesy of Roseburg Timber Products.

Many factors go into weighing how a tree will fall. A skilled faller takes care to lay the tree so as to prevent it splitting or breaking and to minimize damage to residual trees. Broken or split timber is lost revenue.

These men take great pride in their ability to spot where the tree is to land and having it land true.

Simultaneous with the cry of "Timber!" at the moment the tree is set to plunge, those working nearby cease work and turn their heads. Hankering for eyes in the back of their heads, they remain unsure of which way to look. With all senses heightened, they stand at attention keeping a sharp eye on the unpredictable severed tree.

Each man is set to make a hasty dash for safety should faller's miscalculation, a sudden strong gust of wind, or the unexpected rotten or hollow stump put the wrong lean to the tree, and it fails to fall true.

In the event an erratic tree slams headlong into standing timber, there's the danger of being blindsided by a zooming widow-maker.

Though the plummeting tree falls precisely where planned, they can't breathe easy yet. The tons of weight crashing down on the forest floor's ever-present debris of fallen limbs, saplings, and rotting stumps sets in motion another god-awful threat: The dislodged airborne debris and unleashed snapped twigs and snags from the plunging tree are set free to zing through the air in any direction, like arrows shot from a bow.

Even if a person possesses a deer's fleetness of foot and senses honed to a fine edge, anyone near the area is vulnerable to the misery of being clobbered or impaled by a projectile traveling at a sickening rate of speed.

October 13, 1950 *Sutherlin Sun*:

Loss of Eye Due to Previous Logging Accident
Norman 'Dike' Brown . . . underwent an operation at Mercy Hospital ... for the removal of an infected eye.... [His eye was] injured in a logging accident recently, infection set in and the removal was deemed necessary....

JODI OTTEN
Our lady logger of the 1970s, using a 24-inch
Huskie power saw to fall the small timber of the time.

The bucker or buckers take up the job after the tree is down, bucking it into predetermined lengths for skidding to the landing and loading onto the awaiting trucks. This entails not only the actual bucking, but the limbing (removing all limbs) so there is a minimum of drag when skidding the logs to the landing.

Whether working alone or as a team, bucking is one of the more dangerous jobs in the woods. The buckers make every effort to work in "the clear," away from the fallers and out of the line of any maverick falling tree.

Working in small timber, one man does the bucking. Perched atop the fallen unstable tree, he balances his buzzing saw. As he bends over and begins his first cut, the metal caulks of his boots grip the crumbling bark like cats' paws. He must take care and use good judgment to avoid breaking or splintering the tree or injuring himself.

Unlike today's much smaller trees, both in height and girth, during the period of the 1940s-50s mammoth trees were the norm. Bucking them most times called for using the two-man power saw. Because of the lay of the land or the placement of the downed tree, one bucker was forced to work on the downside of an unrestrained tree, which just as likely as not rested on a steep incline.

In either situation, as the bucked log abruptly separates from the rest of the tree, it has the potential to throw the perched logger off balance and roll over him or catch the team bucker working on the log's underside and squash him.

October 4, 1946 *Sutherlin Sun*:

Killed in Woods by Rolling Tree

Dayton Miller...was struck by a rolling tree that had been cut while another tree was falling. [Sic] His injuries consisted of a right chest crushed, broken pelvis bone, and broken right thigh bone. He passed away in the ambulance while being taken to a Eugene Hospital.... He was employed as a faller and bucker....

July 11, 1952 *Sutherlin Sun*:

> Claude B. Dickens, 42, of Sutherlin, was killed Monday when a log he was bucking on a sidehill rolled over him....The log Dickens was bucking had been lodged against a root on the hill. When he sawed off part of it, the other end swung around, knocked him down and rolled over him.

This faller/bucker team is customarily paid a given rate for each thousand board feet of timber cut or scaled, so there is a lack of incentive to work at a leisurely pace.

Aside from performing the actual backbreaking work, wherever these men trudge they are obliged to lug their chain saws with them. Toting around 35 to 50 pounds of deadweight steel up and down rough, litter-strewn terrain, weighted down with the ball and chain of a three-and-one-half pound boot strapped on each foot, is a test of agility. Additionally, being encumbered by the extra burden of the required sledge hammer, razorsharp ax, and steel wedges calls for the upper limit of strength, stamina, and endurance.

From the moment of hoisting the power saw to cutting height until the tree creaks from its stump to begin its descent their work appears effortless. But that is a testament to their strength and skill.

Within the first few days in the woods, many a greenhorn, feeling much like a rejected kamikazi pilot, determines that perhaps he should find another line of work; he just wasn't cut out for this sort of labor.

Skinning the Cat

Most logging performed in Oregon is "sidehill logging," meaning exactly what it implies: logging on rough terrain on the sides of mountains.

Striking out for the day, the cat skinner climbs into his tractor, fires it up, and heads for the nearest logs waiting to be yarded in. After the choker setter hooks the logs onto the cat, the tractor heads back to the landing with its cargo. This process is repeated for the balance of the workday.

SKINNING THE CAT
Cat skidding one giant and one smaller Douglas Fir. Winter Logging Show near Riddle, Oregon, 1949.

The untrod ground the cat plods over may harbor spots of loose soil, thick piles of slick fir needles, or other debris. In the process of moving back and forth across this rough land, the cat skinner comes up against the continual threat of unexpectedly losing traction, thereby opening a Pandora's box of unpleasant surprises.

If the earth gives way beneath its tracks, the bulldozer could dive over, pinning him beneath it. Inching over what would normally be safe small limbs and underbrush, the cat may run up onto a concealed fallen sapling, again causing a loss of traction. This places the cat skinner in the perilous position of losing control of 30 to 40 tons of iron that only moments before he dexterously and skillfully maneuvered along the slope.

Generally, once the cat begins its slide, it's gone—running away and plunging wildly to the bottom of the mountain. Or it may upset, somersaulting end-over-end; or perform hair-raising, acrobatic side rolls until it slams into the nearest immovable obstacle.

As the out-of-control cat gains momentum, knowing when to jump or go for broke and stay with it, is a split-second decision. In most instances, once the cat begins its dizzying descent, the odds of surviving or suffering fewer injuries are enhanced by riding it out— hoping to catch a tree or a stump to stop it, or solid ground where the tracks can bite in and slow its progress.

If the cat is careening sideways, jumping out of its lowside could prove fool-hardy. Should it roll, the operator is directly in its path.

Scrambling over the tilting cat's high side, he stands a chance of escaping by the skin of his teeth. Grabbing onto the topside, he can pull himself up, over, and out of harm's way.

Yet, all things being equal, if the monster machine is skidding straight downward, the frantic operator—getting a quick read on the situation —may make the decision to jump off either side and let it go. The answer is sometimes dependent on the ticklish monetary question of whether you only hired out for wages, or your own hard-earned money is tied up in this costly piece of endangered equipment.

✳   ✳   ✳

Another script may be written whereby the scenario of the successful topside escape from the tilting cat may not play out so well.

Who hasn't taken a short cut or chanced something when in a hurry, thoroughly aware the consequences could cost them dearly? Just this once!

Knowing full well he's flirting with danger, a hardpressed gypo struggling to scratch out a living, tapped out at the bank, and delinquent on his loans has been known to hop into the cat wearing his caulk boots.

Desperation feeds this foolish stunt. In order to cut corners, he and his buddy elect to handle all the work themselves. For a couple of days they've worked at a feverish pace in hopes of delivering several more loads to the mill before the winter rains hit. Now darkness is around the corner. A few more bucks on the check from the mill can head off the bulldozer's repossession. Without that, they're dead in the water.

After they fell and buck several trees, his partner sets chokers as he heads uphill to the cat. Climbing into the machine, he lowers himself into the seat.

Turning the engine over to bring it to life, he assures himself, "It's only a short ways, and in a few minutes I'll be down there. It'll take me that long to get the corks off and my other boots on." And he's probably right. After untying the leather laces from the top pair of eyes, another eighteen hooks need unlacing before he comes to where the laces thread and crisscross through more eyes over his arch. There's still that tangle of laces to loosen before he can tug off the caulks. Then he has to shove his feet into his regular work boots and lace them up.

Manipulating the levers, he begins to navigate the chattering cat downhill to the stump site so he can skid the logs back up to the landing. If the rubber pads have crumbled or worn off the metal foot pedals, its metal pressing against metal with each stop and go. It makes it awkward to run cat, so he'll creep along.

Scary as it is, if the cat pitches sideways and threatens to tumble, and he's forced to scramble out of over the top side, he can kiss his ass goodbye!

As he clumsily fights to gain a foothold to shove off and yank himself out over the high side, the metal spikes embedded in his caulks slip, slide, and scrape against the cat's steel deck, sealing his fate. His efforts are as ineffectual as a basketball player struggling to gain traction on a greased basketball court.

Whistling Past the Graveyard

How treacherous a logging road eventually ends up being is determined by the logging show's location—how sheer and rugged the mountains, and how deep the canyons. Large expenditures on road building are prohibitive for a short-term operation.

Perilously coiling around the mountain, these roads are ordinarily bladed out to be 12 to 14 feet in width at the most. Muscling a truck down these mountain trails, the driver is hemmed in between a steep yawning canyon on one side and the hard unforgiving mountain bank on the other.

During the summer, as day after day, heavy trucks and auxiliary vehicles geehaw up and down the roads, the fine brown dust thickens and grows deeper. As the stirred dust curls up to form billowing clouds, these plumes serve to identify the whereabouts of a loaded truck making its way from the landing. It warns incoming vehicles to utilize the first available turnout to pull over and wait for the loaded truck to ease by.

As stated earlier, if by chance an empty truck comes face-to-face with a loaded log truck on one of these rough paths, the cargo-laden truck, whether headed uphill or down, is afforded the right-of-way.

TOWED
Log truck being towed up hill by cat.
Winter Logging Show near Riddle, Oregon, 1949.

This saddles the unladen truck's driver with the unpleasant task of backing up—either uphill or downhill—to the first available turnout. This puts into force a driving skill unmastered overnight. There are no safe jobs in the woods, and log truck driver is another occupation not for the faint of heart.

* * *

Depending upon the lay of the land, at varying spots along the way a truck could encounter grades of as much as 25 percent. Logging trucks are specifically engineered to be low-geared, which for the most part enables them to pull steep grades. Yet, instances pop up where even an empty rig with its trailer piggybacked on its bunks would be unable to make the grade.

In pulling an exceptionally steep incline, the engine may lose power and cause the truck to stall out. The tires begin to lose traction. There's the smell of rubber as the big wheels spin rapidly, but the truck goes nowhere. With the drive tires spinning ineffectually in the forward direction, the truck's weight and the force of gravity cause it to begin an accelerating backwards slide.

It goes without saying that only an inexperienced driver would place himself or his truck in a precarious situation such as this. Rather, upon reaching an unusually steep incline, a prudent driver with some experience under his belt would stop, signal to the cat skinner by blowing his airhorn, and wait for the operator of the lumbering cat to come to the rescue.

Using a strong steel cable, the cat skinner hooks the truck up to his cat. Slowly but steadily the temporarily disabled truck is towed up the grade to where it can make it under its own power. This negates the likelihood of tearing up drivelines, axles, or a rear end, which are not only expensive to repair but result in downtime and the subsequent loss of earnings.

Truckin' By the Seat of Your Pants

Bill Kenwisher, with his brother Otto, logged in the Sutherlin area in the early 40s. He tells of hauling logs out of Rock Island Camp about 15 miles east of Sutherlin, and at the end of the county road. He described the logging road from there into the landing as being, "six miles of switchbacks straight up and straight down." (Switchbacks are zigzag turns, sharply turning in one direction, then quickly switching back in the opposite direction.)

He went on to remark, "I hauled out of there. It was called Rock Island Hill."

His truck and trailer were equipped with the standard, but unreliable vacuum brakes. "There was air [brakes], but no water on 'em."

In the heat of summer, fear rode as a passenger each day as they confronted the chilling possibility that snaking down that winding steep grade their brakes might overheat, triggering the grim reality of brake failure.

He recalled, "At that time, there wasn't the luxury of trucks equipped with power steering, and herding those rigs up and down those roads was done by 'armstrong steering.' It was truckin' by the seat of your pants."

* * *

In the early 1950s the newer model log trucks came equipped with air brakes and had a water tank mounted behind the cab. The tank was pressurized by air from the truck compressor forcing water through rubber hoses onto the brake drums. This prevented brakes from overheating.

For that time period these innovations were the foremost safety features designed and installed on log trucks. Although air brakes decreased many of the perils inherent in trucks making their way out of the woods, on the other hand it presented a new danger to chill the spine—the hidden and insidious loss of air to the air brakes while descending down a winding, menacing grade.

The rubber air hoses (also called air lines) that supplied air to the brakes were suspended under the trailing log trailer's reach pole that attached to the truck's frame. At that time the usual length of Douglas fir hauled was 42 feet; therefore, the wooden reach pole extended 30 feet out from the front of the log trailer.

Despite every care taken to secure and tie these lines in place, when the truck and trailer were loaded there remained a certain amount of slack in the lines. This slack allowed the truck to negotiate its trailer around sharp turns without snapping the lines.

Lying in places along the road's surface were beds of loose, sharp rock or the remains of tree roots. As day after day the heavily loaded rigs moved over these rutted trails, the ruts grew deeper. Little by little the reach pole and air hoses inched closer to the ground. If the air hoses reached the point where they began to drag the ground, they were now set to catch on any protruding root or centered rock. The snagged hose could quietly snap, giving no hint of its severed condition until the brakes were applied on the next downgrade, and the oblivious trucker came to the frightening realization that there were none.

In a heartbeat, the driver must assess his options and grapple with the unenviable dilemma of whether he should optimistically bail out, which few drivers survived, or scrapping that idea, swallow hard and ride it on out to its conclusion, praying that he retain some semblance of control.

If at all familiar with his surroundings, he might conjure up an image of a spot in the road or a place angling off from it, where he stood a chance to slow the runaway or bring it to a quick grinding halt.

1926 LOGGING TRUCK
Taken on bridge near Jennings, Oregon.
The truck was owned by Ken Ford's father, Clair Ford.
Photograph courtesy of Roseburg Timber Products.

Otherwise, looking as though his time had run out, the driver was on his own—either to end up helplessly slamming into a tree or the side of the mountain, plummeting straight off a hairpin curve into the waiting canyon's void, or miraculously completing a wild, nerve-shattering ride to the bottom.

May 13, 1949 *Sutherlin Sun*:

> George Robert Chartier, 33, was carried to his death Friday when his log truck got out of control and careened down a steep logging road 20 miles east of Sutherlin....The truck's brakes failed to hold, and the loaded vehicle sped 800-900 yards before crashing into a tree. The logs slid forward and crushed the driver's compartment....

Every summer would see at least one fatality or shattering injury among the log haulers caused by a roaring out-of-control truck.

Ironically, the fatality was not necessarily that of the driver, but of a fellow worker who happened to be in the wrong place at the wrong time.

May 31, 1946 *Sutherlin Sun*:

> John Alfred Ellis, 30, was killed in the woods when hit by a logging truck while working in the Martin Bros. timber tract on Coon Creek early last Friday morning, May 24, 1946.

Is That All There Is?

Seeing that the funeral had already taken place, the above one-liner brought to a close the account of John Ellis's untimely demise: end of story. Finis!

This weekly hometown newspaper supplied no further details as to how the accident occurred. Nor, would there be a followup in next week's paper because by then, inevitably there would be another death or bloody accident to report. His death didn't justify the typesetter's big bold headlines at the top of the page as did the really big news of the week: the upcoming Father's day feed, and the Women's Temperance Union meeting scheduled for June 11th.

The hard-to-bear truth was that the hot news of who went shopping in Eugene the previous week; or the write-up about so-and-so's baby shower, including naming all 15 women in attendance, and who won a prize—along with the scoop on who motored from out of town—deserved more ink.

The brief account of John Ellis's passing did give his birthplace and named his survivors. By way of bestowing a small bit of recognition of his worth and status, it was noted, "he had served in the U.S. Army during the War."

There can be no doubt that after being mustered out of the Army, both he and his family rejoiced at his safe return. Yet, less than a year later, while working in a peacetime industry that proved to be about as dangerous as front-line service, his all-too-short life was snuffed out.

Did John Ellis suffer a war injury that slowed down his reaction time? Was it inattentiveness on someone's part that led to his being hit by a log truck? What was the story?

It would have been noteworthy to mention what rank he'd attained in the service, in what battles he'd fought, or what medals he may have earned. It would appear the poor fellow was just a foot soldier whose life didn't amount to a hill of beans. Or, was it that he was just another casualty of the woods?

The lack of any specifics about his death was not that unusual. The reporting of logging accidents and fatalities were ofttimes sketchy. They were treated as everyday incidents.

But every so often there was the harrowing story to be told of the successful jump from a cat, truck, or some other rampaging piece of equipment, or the account given from a hospital bed about an unnerving roller coaster ride to the bottom of a canyon.

These close brushes with death were always good for anecdotes to be told and retold with a mixture of exhilaration and bravado in the bars after work, and for many years later as "the one that got away."

CHAPTER SIX

The Post War Army's Million-Dollar-A-Day Habit

At war's end in 1945, the timber industry had proved to be a crucial cog in the wheel of the war machine. That year, loggers in Douglas County cut 518 million board feet of timber resulting in lumber production of 382 million board feet. But that still was insufficient to fill the bill.

The cry for lumber did not decrease, it increased. That was brought about because of the immediate and urgent demand for housing to meet the needs of returning servicemen and their families, and to fill the pentup demand for postponed commercial construction. In February of 1946 the West Coast Lumber Industry scrambled to produce enough lumber for the building of 500,000 homes, but found that much of it was being diverted to deferred commercial construction.

Being faulted for hanging back and failing to produce sufficient lumber, the Lumber Manufacturing Industry denied that they were responsible for the housing shortage. Rightfully defensive, they cited the useless building of race tracts, roadhouses, saloons, pool rooms, dance halls, and gambling joints as being the true reason for this lumber shortfall. They charged, "The veteran and his family who want a new home stand at the end of a long line of customers for construction." This situation was recognized as the reason the Civilian Production Administration and the National Housing Agency handed down an order to immediately divert materials from commercial construction to the imperative business of home building.

Ranch-style and split-level houses sprang up across the countryside as fast as they could be built. These developments, filled with "tickytacky little boxes" all in a row, were the inspiration for the 1950s song bearing that title.

According to Ellis Lucia, author of *Head Rig* mentioned in the last chapter, in six years the United States purchased and consumed 215 billion board feet of lumber. This came from timber logged from at least 10 million acres of our forests. And despite the cessation of the war, in 1946 the U.S. Army competed with the relentless civilian demand by spending approximately a million dollars a day for this precious commodity.

Sutherlin's population continued to swell, but the severe shortage of workers persisted. The first returning servicemen came home to fill the awaiting jobs in the woods and, without fanfare, to displace the plucky women who had been holding down the sawmill jobs. Picking up their last paychecks, without even an "Attagirl", the women understood the implied message: "Ladies, you're no longer needed, return to your kitchens."

Indicative of the opportunities awaiting men eager to work was the overnight growth of sawmills. Like service stations, they sprouted up on every corner; not only large mills expected to employ several hundred men, but the small family-run mills. In 1945, according to the West Coast Lumbermen's Association statistics, Douglas County boasted 89 sawmills; a year later, almost doubling, there were 167.

That same year, responding to the goading, hounding, and incessant prodding for more lumber, Douglas County loggers proved their mettle by single-handedly increasing production over 1945's logging output by another 200 million board feet.

All this increased productivity came at a high price. For the first five postwar years, 1946 through 1950, 288 Oregon loggers were killed. and 90 Oregon sawmill workers met their demise on the job. This adds up to a sobering statistic of 378 Oregon timber workers killed in that five-year period. This breaks down to a gutwrenching statistic of 75 Oregon timber workers killed annually trying to keep up with the postwar demand.

Did anyone march on city hall or the state capital demanding an end to this slaughter? Did any lofty organization or individuals set up a hue and cry for the timber industry to slow down? Did anyone question if that lumber, supposedly needed to satisfy civilian demands, justified the human price tag? I don't think so.

This cost fails to take into account the heartbreaking loss of sight and limbs. There is no record of the hundreds of maiming and crippling injuries resulting from this frenzied production.

Those heroic loggers and mill workers had a job to do, and they did it damn well.

CHAPTER SEVEN

Weyerhauser's Entry Into Sutherlin

The seemingly boundless and inexhaustible timberlands surrounding Sutherlin held a staggering inventory of unharvested logs and unmilled lumber. With the shortfall in lumber production, it was worth its weight in gold. Making public its intention to locate a logging camp and set up operations in the area, Weyerhaeuser Timber Company became a big player in the new gold rush.

It was to be several years down the road, specifically January of 1949, before logging could begin. The announced site of these operations was 17 miles east of Sutherlin, at what was referred to as Camp Sutherlin.

Prior to the commencement of logging operations and before any logs could be moved, Weyerhaeuser first had to build a railroad. Track had to be laid from Sutherlin eastward those 17 miles to where its mammoth timber holdings began. This would allow the logs to be transported by rail into town and then transferred onto the Southern Pacific Railroad. Thereafter, the logs would be shipped to Weyerhaeuser's large and newly constructed mill pond in Springfield, Oregon, for eventual processing through its pulp mill and sawmill located on the same property.

The initial announcement of Weyerhaeuser's plans was music to the ears of the townspeople as well as the city fathers. Right away the company launched a program of positive public relations so as to expediently acquire all necessary rights-of-way.

Because of Weyerhaeuser's decision to build a railroad, it proved an opportune time for the town to initiate a few political maneuvers for its benefit. The city needed an improved water system, and it just so happened that the rail line would run alongside the city's reservoir. At one point during grade construction it was acknowledged that a certain amount of rock would end up in the city reservoir.

OLD STEAM ENGINE #100, 1950s
Traveling from Camp Sutherlin into Sutherlin.
Photograph courtesy of Weyerhaeuser Archives, Tacoma, Washington.

Since the company sought the townsfolk's goodwill, members of the City Council exploited the opportunity and applied subtle pressure in seeking its assistance to bankroll an improved water system. This was disclosed in a Weyerhaeuser inter-office memo dated September 11, 1947, reporting on a City Council meeting held earlier.

To present themselves as good neighbors, they could not outright refuse to work with the city and to make every effort to mitigate any contamination of the reservoir.

Quoting from this memo:

> The City Council...has realized for some time that they need an improved water system at Sutherlin to take care of their increased population. They raised the water assessment a year ago and have this year been able to set aside $20,000 looking toward the installation of a new filter plant or whatever is necessary.

> They have apparently seized upon a small amount of rock which we must put into their reservoir as an excuse to tap us for as much as they can get from us to aid them in the development of a better water system.

Stressing the company's need for good public relations, the City Council repeatedly asked what cooperation they could expect.

Soft-pedaling the issue, it was jointly agreed that if the city's water system required support by the industries around Sutherlin that they should be canvassed to determine their support, and Weyerhaeuser "would consider a donation at that time on its merits."

In the end, the City accepted Weyerhaeuser's offer of engineering assistance in planning a better water system—and with a change of plans, agreed to bypass a rock cut that would have dumped rock into the reservoir.

By all manner of means, Weyerhaeuser became a good neighbor, and its presence in the area contributed immensely to Sutherlin's already surging economy.

To begin the Sutherlin operation, their budgeted equipment expenditure for 1948 was $414,500; this included the cost of a diesel locomotive and a caboose. Road construction equipment was excluded from this amount, with the projection that the following year it would be necessary to spend another $75,000 for that equipment.

The purchase of the budgeted diesel engine was tabled for a time. Instead, after completion of the railroad, Weyerhaeuser put into service an old steam engine that it acquired in 1948.

On January 16, 1949, Old Engine 100, the number proudly emblazoned in white on its front, and its railcars piled high with freshly felled logs, set out on its maiden journey into town. Winding and rattling its way through the hills and valley along the newly laid track, it traversed at least ten bridges that crossed over the many streams emptying into the Calapooya River. An historical report of this "little engine that could" was given in a February, 1980 *Ruralite* article by Seabe Calhoun:

> The log cars were neatly loaded at the transfer landing by Johnny Gaines and his crew. They stacked the logs in the metal bunks until the logs peaked at about nine feet. A full load for the train would be at least 25 cars; sometimes as many as 60 made the run...

> Old 100, like all steam locomotives, was always ready to go. It was seldom allowed to get cold because it took at least eight hours to bring it up to steam.

This reliable little engine performed nobly up through the early 1950's when it was forced into a meritable retirement and replaced by the diesel previously put on the back burner.

The Camp

A good brief summarization of Camp Sutherlin was given by J. F. Hollandsworth in an interview for the Weyerhaeuser Timber Company Archives. (Forrest Hollandsworth took over as logging foreman of the camp in the fall of 1949, and the following year became its superintendent.)

> Had a camp for about eleven families and a cookhouse and bunkhouse to serve about 50 people. Generally had around 30 people. In those days, people were very hard to get. So hired about everybody that came on. Really, we were our own personnel people at that time. We didn't give physicals. We just about took what came in and put them to work. To say the least, the help for the most part was not too good to start with. The logging camp was 17 miles east of Sutherlin on a gravel road. Throughout the winter times, it was impassable for three or four days a week. Electricity was just about as erratic. We did without the electricity throughout the winter just about a quarter of the time. We had a D.C. power plant that furnished electricity for the cookhouse and the bunkhouses, but as far as the Company houses, we were kind of on our own. We had our gas lanterns, candles, and whatever it took.

> Not too much social life in camp, other than visiting back and forth with the people that lived there. Quite a few kids in camp. Really a pretty good place for the kids to get their start. Had timber—kind of a little park—all around them, right on a creek. In the summer, we took our tractors and dammed the creek up on the weekend. We just got the tractor right in the middle of the creek and pushed the rock up and made our own swimming hole.

Reflecting back to that time, Mr. Hollandsworth recalls one old fellow they hired early on who had "heart trouble and bum legs and a bum back and just about everything that could be wrong with a guy." It seems that the company acquired a right-of-way through his homestead to build its road and railroad. After having time to rethink the situation, the gentleman became quite distressed and believed Weyerhaeuser had taken unfair advantage of him.

Hollandsworth said, "He later thought he had made a bum deal and sat out there with his rifle to stop all traffic." Representatives tried to

reason with him, but couldn't. They then offered him a job, giving new meaning to the expression, "If you can't beat 'em, join 'em."

Fortunately, after accepting the job offer, the irate landowner performed well despite his disabilities. He worked right up to the time Weyerhaeuser closed their operations at Sutherlin.

Playing it Safe

During that era of few government mandated safety regulations, safety in the woods was nonetheless of paramount concern for all loggers and most logging operators. No employer deliberately took a callous attitude towards safety, but production many times placed higher on the priority scale.

Locally, Weyerhaeuser Timber maintained one of the best safety records in the logging industry due, no doubt, to its having the financial resources to outfit its equipment with the latest and best innovations designed to protect workers.

Additionally, the company possessed the wherewithal to supply its employees with whatever gear or guidance might be needed to mitigate the risks and dangers naturally inherent in their work environment.

To that end, all employees at one time or another were required to take first aid training. Knowing how to stop further blood loss right at the job sight by the proper application of a tourniquet was crucial. It could literally mean the difference between life and death. The wearing of protective headgear, introduced into the shipyards during the war, appeared to make just as much sense for men in the woods. Weyerhaeuser became the first employer in the area to require its employees to wear hard hats. This requirement, however, was met with resentment and a lot of bitching. The men protested donning what they called "helmets" or "tin hats" and admitted that wearing them made them feel foolish.

CREW AT WEYERHAEUSER CAMP
(*Left and Below*) Sutherlin, July 1956.
Forrest Rehwalt is second from left in the photograph below.
Photograph courtesy of Forrest Rehwalt, Springfield, Oregon.

Bill Baird who worked at Camp Sutherlin recalls, "I hated it, and the others grumbled about it, particularly the equipment operators who saw no need for them."

One of the advantages Weyerhaeuser's truck drivers enjoyed was the luxury of driving over their well-maintained, gravelled mainline logging roads.

Also, the majority of its privately owned and operated off-highway logging trucks came equipped with air brakes, while many of the hardpressed gypos made do with the old unreliable hydraulic and vacuum brakes.

A cut above the others, the company held the distinction of being the only employer around to have an ambulance housed at the work site and at the ready when needed.

Before the acquisition of its ambulance, an ambulance had to be summoned out of Roseburg. This emergency run to camp could take 45 minutes depending on the condition of Nonpareil Road. Making matters worse, it wouldn't be unusual for 15 precious minutes to have elapsed from the time of the accident to the injured worker's arrival by stretcher at the main camp.

After the ambulance doors slammed shut, the painwracked victim must tough out a harrowing 17 mile ride over the chuck-hole-pitted dirt and gravel road just to reach town. In most cases, Dr. Grabow would be unequipped to handle the case, and the ambulance driver would have to white-knuckle it on to a hospital in either Roseburg or Eugene.

The patient's life hung in the balance, and it would be touch and go whether he survived long enough to make it to a hospital. Time was of the essence, and with logging injuries, your grim enemy.

Despite every precaution taken and every innovation made, the company incurred its share of accidents. The truth of the matter is, especially in the woods, that no divine way exists for planning or anticipating every unforeseen contingency or insidious lurking hazard.

For any logger, the mere act of showing up for work indicated a certain willingness to risk your neck. And the longer your time in the woods, the greater the certainty of the unfavorable odds catching up with you.

Caught in the Bite of the Line

It began as a typical workday for Weyerhaeuser's employees. For the men living in town, it started long before daybreak. After arriving there by foot or by car, they huddled or mingled around in front of the school's gymnasium building. This site on the eastern edge of town was the designated spot for Weyerhaeuser's crummy (in this case an old refurbished school bus) to pick them up each day.

The sleepy-eyed men, a few groggily sipping the last of a cup of coffee, clutched their weighty jam-packed lunch pails as they talked among themselves. Some visited, some groused.

When the crummy showed up, they piled on for their trip out of town to the company's operations. Their ride terminated at the camp itself, which housed the administrative offices as well as the company-supplied housing

Arriving in the gray early morning quiet, the sun not yet making its appearance, they were afforded a picture-postcard view of the camp. It nestled in a cleared area giving the clipped and clean appearance of a park. It was surrounded by the inhabitants' workplace: the dense majestic forests.

All the lighted houses and buildings, including the bunkhouses and cookhouse, were neatly painted white with contrasting green trim. In the background the soothing murmur of the crystal-clear creek fell upon the ear as it meandered and gurgled alongside the camp. From the lighted cookhouse, smoke curled from the chimney to rise and mingle with the delicate fragrance of fir and cedar trees.

Inside the welcoming cookhouse, the harried cook and kitchen helper rushed to complete the serving of a hot and hearty breakfast to anywhere from 30 to 50 robust hungry men. These were the men who called the bunkhouses home.

After the men shoved their plates aside and their chairs back, a worker hustled to clear off the tables. Working behind the cleanup, another helper began laying out a variety of freshly cooked meats, sandwich spreads, and breads. To top off this smorgasbord, he set out an appetizing assortment of cookies, cakes, and fresh fruits. This spread allowed the bunkhouse boarders to go whole hog and cram their lunch buckets with all the grub they wanted. This would have to get them through a long day's work. They knew all too well that what they neglected to take with them would be unavailable elsewhere.

These abundantly prepared foods were not yesterday's tired leftovers, but had been whipped up especially for their lunches. Sometimes the city fellas wandering in for a quick gulp of coffee gazed upon their counterparts' bill of fare with envious eyes.

Maybe it applied to cowboys, but the men living in these bunkhouses were not treated as hired hands, but instead more as prima donnas. This held true especially where it concerned their afterhours comfort and meals. Here, after the work day ended, they enjoyed a feast of all they could eat, a hot shower, a clean bed, the sociability of their fellow workers, and a few hands of cards. Not a bad life at all!

As Forrest Hollandsworth, camp superintendent, stated, "Pretty good to have a cookhouse in those days because you couldn't get enough people that lived around there to work... wasn't available people to work. So we used the bunkhouse/cookhouse situation to get people."

From this picturesque base of operations, both the men from town and those who bunked there were divided up and dispersed to their individual logging sides—again riding the distance in Weyerhaeuser's

bright yellow crummies (also known as man wagons). Each side was a separate logging show identified as the 200 Line, the 300 Line, and the 500 Line.

Camp Sutherlin's main road ran about five miles out from camp and was kept in good shape. This was known as the Main Line Road. The numbered Lines were logically determined by the spot where each one-lane dirt logging road veered off from this Main Line Road. The 200 Line was reached by departing the main road approximately two miles from camp, making a sharp turn and proceeding up the mountain three-and-one-half miles to that logging show.

The 300 and 500 Lines also left the main road three and five miles respectively from camp. After turning off the Main Line Road at either diverging point, the crummies bounced and rattled along over the graveled dirt trails back into the boondocks to that logging show.

On this particular day, the workaday sounds of the incessant buzzing of power saws, the droning of log trucks shifting through their gears as they wound up or down the roads, and the chattering of the yarder skidding logs all dueled for attention as they echoed through the forest.

The men working on the 200 Line busied themselves as the loading donkey skidded the immense logs up to the landing. These were being winched in from down below where just moments before choker setters finished up wrapping and securing the chokers around them.

With no hint of trouble, the young company foreman, Kenneth Dice, absentmindedly watched the work in progress. The clattering yarder labored as it winched in its tethered logs. Immersed in his own thoughts, he failed to notice that the haulback line (5/8" steel-core wire rope), which is attached to the main cable running from the spar tree and secured around the logs, had become ensnared on a three-foot high stump. This put a tremendous strain on the line.

All at once the cable dislodged itself and with lightening speed slid up over the top of the stump, snapping back into a straight line with terrifying force. The unbridled snapping power and weight of the cable hit the unsuspecting foreman with such a jarring and explosive impact that his hard hat became partially embedded into his skull, killing him on the spot.

Weyerhaeuser required all crummies to carry a radio and stretcher. One of the men dashed to the crummy and radioed the main office while another grabbed the stretcher. Forrest Rehwalt, Wayne Hall and two others loaded Ken Dice onto the stretcher and into the crummy and raced to camp. This accident occurred before Weyerhaeuser had its own ambulance, so one was summoned from Roseburg. Since that ambulance hadn't arrived yet and every minute counted, they gunned the crummy on towards town. Not too far out, they met up with the screeching ambulance and transferred the foreman into it.

The May 2, 1952 *Sutherlin Sun* reported that Kenneth Dice, 37, died "...as a result of injuries received in a logging accident earlier in the day... he was admitted for treatment of a fractured skull... after presumably being struck by a haulback line."

Whether with sinking heart, the yarder operator shouted a warning to the foreman, or if he caught him in his line of vision at all, is unknown. In all probability, even if he did his best to call out to him, it is doubtful that he'd have been heard over the din of the various surging engines powering the equipment; at least not in time for Dice to drop to the ground or scramble to safety. This kind of accident takes place often enough to have a specific term ascribed to it—"caught in the bite of the line."

The occurrence of such a sobering accident on a logging show where you worked reinforced a respect for the gauntlet of risks run every day. After any fatality, on any show, it took several days for the men to put it out of their minds and resume their normal workaday routines. It served as a chilling reminder—just in case you'd become a little less vigilant or a slight bit careless. And this one really hit home.

WEYERHAEUSER CAMP, 1950S
Logging in progress on the 200 Line. Superintendent Forrest Hollandsworth is seen in the foreground.
Photograph courtesy of Forrest Rehwalt.

Making One's Way

Within a week's time following this tragedy, his own vulnerability still fresh on his mind, Dode Winter hoisted himself up into his rig. He was all set for his usual morning venture back into the woods from the Camp Sutherlin rallying point. For the past year, the tall, slender 24-year-old had worked as a truck driver at Weyerhaeuser.

After his discharge from the service, he was footloose and fancy free, so he struck out for that part of the country. He'd heard of the employment opportunities that awaited a young man unopposed to hard work. While he was away, his parents had taken up residence in Sutherlin, so he knew he'd at least have a place to stay.

The house and service station his folks purchased occupied the same piece of property, and they managed the station by themselves. Knowing a good thing when they saw it, since it was off Highway 99 with sufficient parking space for trucks, they catered to the log truck traffic.

For the four years prior to hiring on with Weyerhaeuser, Dode worked as a cat skinner and truck driver for several gypo loggers and had no bones to pick with either job. Seemingly always cheerful with an everready laugh, he got along with everyone. He loved the outdoor work and couldn't imagine anyone who wouldn't.

Aside from the recent fatality, Dode had become all too familiar with the dangers of working in the woods—since two of his brothers logged in the Sutherlin vicinity. He'd been working for them the day his oldest brother, Bud, made a hairbreadth escape with his life. While felling a tree, Bud was caught off guard when the toppling tree unpredictably "came back over the stump," violently smashing into him and pinning him to the ground.

The phrase "coming back over the stump" describes what occurs when a severed tree fails to fall as intended — plunging straight downward, with the bottom of the cut tree first poised vertically and remaining directly over the stump, then leaning towards and eventually falling in the intended direction. But, rather by some quirk of fate, miscalculation, or act of God, the toppling tree in its downward fall may split, or the accelerating momentum may cause the severed butt end to kick back without warning, hurtling it off the stump and slamming it headlong into the hapless faller.

Luckily for Bud, the tree didn't hit him dead center, but caught his left side as it crashed downward. After helping to lift his unconscious brother into his car, Dode raced for the hospital in Roseburg. Since they were logging west of town beyond the Umpqua Store, this involved about an 18-mile drive speeding over a graveled back road. For most of the trip, the speedometer needle sat on 80 mph, the best his car would do.

In addition to the trauma and multiple bruises, Bud suffered a serious concussion, and most of the muscles and tendons in his left arm were severed. For four of his days in the hospital he remained unconscious. Following an operation to repair the mangled arm, he made a good recovery despite a poor prognosis.

This race against time validates another cardinal rule loggers live by: never drive to work on a near-empty gas tank with the intention of filling it up on the way home! On any day, when least expected, yours may be the vehicle commandeered to do duty as an emergency ambulance. If you've come to grief and your luck's run out, fate may decree that it's you that gets shoved into the back seat for a hair-raising ride to the nearest hospital.

The Escape Ramp

Except for it being uncommonly warm for May, the day began as any other. With his trailer piggybacked on his truck, Winter headed out

LOADED LOG TRUCK
Weyerhaeuser Company off-highway log truck.
Sutherlin operations, 1950s.
Photograph courtesy of Weyerhaeuser Archives, Tacoma, Washington.

to the 500 Line for his first load of the day. Five miles out from camp he made a sharp turn off the Main Line Road and drove six more looping, winding miles up to the logging show atop the mountain. At this point, all the merchantable timber on this mountain had been logged off.

As he pulled into the landing, he was greeted by the alto roar of the operating heavy-duty, diesel-powered equipment. He dropped his trailer and hitched it up to the truck for loading.

The landing crew scurried about earning their money. This was a high-lead show using a rigged spar pole and yarder. The yarder operator occupied himself with the job at hand, bringing in a turn of logs.

This specific landing sat back at the furthest passable distance from the Weyerhaeuser Camp. Scanning the horizon in any direction from this vantage point, there was no hint of civilization—no town, no small community, not even a simple log cabin. It staggered the imagination. For as far as the eye could see, stretching to the endless horizon, stood magnificent, untouched virgin timberlands encompassing thousands of acres. No matter how often he took it in, Winter couldn't help being awestruck.

Unnoticed while loading the logs, the loader operator shortsightedly placed a log that had a stubby, fairly sharp limb jutting from it onto the bunks of the truck and trailer. These bunks carry the weight of the logs.

The placement of this mischief-making log allowed the sharp limb to protrude down through the open area of the trailer frame. No one had any idea that this jagged limb had snapped off the drain valve on the air-reserve tank that feeds the truck's air system. The function of the drain valve is to allow foreign elements, such as water and possibly oil, to be drained out of the air system.

At that time, Dode noticed no loss of air pressure to the brake system or any hint of a problem. The limb completely covered and hid from view the gaping hole and, for the moment, allowed the air to remain in the system.

Since these logs were loaded on an off-highway truck with over-width bunks (only to be driven to the transfer landing and loaded onto rail-cars), the load was not tied down with the customary chains and binders. Instead, the logs were loaded so as to stay cradled and balanced on the eighteen-wheeler. Upon reaching the company railroad and transfer station, the logs would be offloaded as one unit and transferred to a waiting rail-car.

After easing away from the level landing, he maneuvered the loaded rig the short distance to the mountain's edge. There, Winter, as was his routine, stopped the truck, set the air brakes, and turned on the valves that sent water to the brakes. Alighting from the cab, he paid close attention as he went about a wheel-to-wheel inspection of the eight rear wheels on the truck and an equal number on the trailer. He checked to be certain there was a good strong water flow to all brake drums. In the process of performing this safety check, he kept a sharp, trained ear out for any ominous hissing leaks or air emitting from the air pressure system.

No experienced driver would attempt to descend this long a downgrade without first doing this step-by-step safety check. For that matter, no driver worth his salt would attempt a descent down any substantial downgrade, no matter how short, without being certain his safety systems were fully functional.

Reassured, Dode returned to the idling truck and pulled himself up into the cab. Getting comfortable, he shifted down into low gear and began the approach to the narrow one-lane primitive road chopped out of the mountainside. Taking it easy, he edged his beast of burden off the mountain to commence the slow downhill journey. Before returning to the relative safety of the Main Line Road, there was a six-mile downgrade to navigate.

As the truck made the first turn, this also turned the trailer, which is designed to trail in a direct line behind the truck. In so doing, this changed the angle of the bunks and, no one the wiser, caused the limb to move off the broken drain valve. This exposed the ruptured hole and allowed the air to the air brakes to escape. Engineered to maintain 120 PSI (pounds per square inch) air pressure, these air systems came equipped with a warning buzzer set to go off at 60 PSI.

With the safety of your airlines being your lifeline, over time Winter developed the habit of keeping an anxious eye on his air pressure gauge. A short second before he found it necessary to apply his brakes, he couldn't believe his eyes. The damn air gauge needle was falling fast! He heard himself blurt out, "Holy Shit!" as he hit his brakes, but the truck was unresponsive. There was no slowing it. A sudden sinking sick feeling overwhelmed him. He'd lost his air on a steep downgrade, a trucker's worst nightmare.

At the moment of the futile application of the brakes, the warning buzzer sounded. But this ominous buzzing caused no additional alarm as the adrenalin had been flowing from the instant he saw the gauge's falling needle. He knew he was in big trouble. As a matter of fact, he was dead in the water if he didn't keep a cool head. Everything hinged on his remaining in control of the truck by whatever means he could dream up. He'd have to take advantage of whatever minute opportunity came his way. It looked like he was in for the ride of his life.

In his mind's eye, he visualized a fork in the road about a quarter of a mile further downhill. There, a similar crude dirt trail branched off to the left at about a 45-degree angle and followed a steep incline back up the hill. If he could maintain control of the truck and negotiate a detour up that rough grade, he could slow the truck and bring it to a gradual stop.

With his brakes gone, he had to rely on the compression generated by the engine to rein in the truck and maintain a slow enough speed to coast down to his make-do escape ramp.

RELOAD STATION AT SPRINGFIELD OPERATIONS
Logs were transferred from trucks onto railcars. Sutherlin's operations were identical to Springfield.
Photograph courtesy of Weyerhaeuser Archives, Tacoma, Washington.

Showing its distress, the truck began to whine in low gear. This torturous complaining could be expected in its task of holding back the natural acceleration of 50 tons of truck and logs on a steep downgrade. The worrisome whine soon grew more urgent, indicating that the laboring engine was revved up to its maximum RPM.

In order to protect the engine and prevent its blowup, thereby causing the total loss of compression, Winter instinctively upshifted two gears. At this point, to attempt upshifting only one gear would be foolhardy. The mere disengaging of the clutch to shift would allow the truck to flatout gain speed. Therefore, to both ward off damage to the engine and attain the best payback for the momentum gathered during the clutch disengagement, he must swiftly and skillfully upshift two gears. And pray that he could synchronize this smoothly and with no hesitation. His timing must be flawless!

This doubletime upshifting would permit the truck to travel at a faster speed, yet maintain a lower engine RPM and sufficient compression to prevent a complete runaway.

The same scenario of dangerous engine over-revving and jamming up two gears repeated itself. But by now Winter felt reassured that, despite his unsafe speed, both he and the renegade truck would make it all in one piece to the stop-gap destination.

*   *   *

With most of the timber harvested clear to the bottom of the mountain, from his position he had an unobstructed downward view of the road. At about the same moment he heaved a sigh of relief, confident that he'd reach his safe haven, he was hit by a sight that popped out the goose bumps and retied his stomach into a spasm of knots.

"Sonofabitch!"

He couldn't believe his eyes—nor his bad luck. One of the company's bright yellow pickups (painted so for apparent reasons) had just come into view and was winding its way up the mountain. And it was within a short distance of his planned detour.

Winter knew the pickup driver couldn't help but see his truck descending downhill, but feared he might fail to pay attention to the downward-bound truck's excessive speed.

Since the "Rule of the Road" dictated the upward-bound vehicle to pull over into the first available turnout, Winter cursed his bad luck. It was cut and dried that the pickup's destined turnout would more than likely be Winter's predetermined runaway truck ramp. With his heart in his throat, Dode laid on the airhorn fed by a now feeble buildup of air. It was imperative that he get the unsuspecting pickup driver's attention so that he realize that the downward-bound truck was in a runaway mode.

It was a toss of the dice. Would the foreman driving the pickup discern the problem? And if he did, would he have the presence of mind to reason that the driver of the runaway would most likely use the diverging road as an escape ramp? If the driver failed to read it right, Winter was caught between the proverbial rock and a hard spot. He didn't stand a ghost of a chance of coming out of this unscathed.

His mind spun as he conjured up and worked through his two options. If the pickup driver used the roughed-out grade for a turnout, he was screwed. He could take a long shot and go for it, but at his speed and with all the weight he carried behind him, neither of them stood a snowball's chance in hell of surviving the ensuing crash.

His second alternative would be to hang tough and take his chances by herding the raging monster on down the hill. He'd have to let her rip until he and the truck ended up in a tangled heap of twisted metal, the load of logs heaped helterskelter upon and around him. He could choose to do it either at the hand-picked spot with the foreman—an option he'd shitcanned—or randomly at another.

Fortunately, the pickup driver read all the danger signals and hit upon Dode's logical course of action. He pulled his pickup off to the side of the road and stopped.

But the bad dream wasn't over yet. He'd parked it just short of the makeshift road. It sat in such close proximity to the fork that Winter feared that in negotiating the sharp detour the truck's momentum could conceivably propel the unsecured logs directly onto the pickup and driver.

The normal safe speed for a loaded log truck down this particular grade was five to seven miles per hour. Winter estimated his speed in turning into the uphill exit somewhere between 30 and 35 miles per hour. As he made the tight curve and lurched past the pickup, he recalls vividly seeing the terrified driver's "eyes as big as saucers," as he sat frozen in the seat of his pickup holding his breath while the truck navigated the sharp turn with its cargo intact.

This ungraded detouring road was in the process of being forged back into another remote area and had only been roughed out by a bulldozer. It was full of dirt piles, good-sized boulders and smaller rocks, and chuck holes of varying depths. As the driver struggled to keep the truck under control, he bounced and tossed around in the cab like a rubber ball, his hard hat banging and clanging against the cab's metal top. Erratically bounding up the incline, the truck steadily slowed, shuddered, and wrapped in a cloud of dust, came to a jerking halt.

Exhilarated at beating the odds, Dode couldn't help but smile to himself at his first conscious thought: "Damn, that tin hat DID come in handy!"

Two unnerved, badly shaken but elated drivers emerged from their respective vehicles. Laughing nervously and shaking their heads, they jointly heaved sighs of relief.

As the dust settled and the last rocks tumbled down the canyon, you could hear the sigh emitting from the wayward truck; or was it merely the last gasp of air belching from the broken air valve?

As the day ended, the grimy and weary men piled into the crummies for the drive back to the main camp. In keeping with a hardandfast rule, every man must be accounted for. No man is left to work alone in the woods, on any logging show, for any reason.

From the camp, the loggers from town, grasping now empty lunch buckets, their dusty and wrinkled jackets tossed over tired shoulders, loaded back onto the old bus for their homeward ride. If it had been a long day, the moon would be coming up about the time they got back to town, the reason some have referred to a logger's work-day as "two moonlight rides and a picnic lunch."

Tomorrow would be another day—not like today and not like yesterday—as fate will take charge and the script for tomorrow rewritten. Whatever its tale, you can be assured it will be neither tediously routine nor dull, but unpredictable and rife with challenge, where an error in judgment, or an omission, has an incalculable cost.

PART THREE

THE TOWN'S CLOCKWORKS

CHAPTER EIGHT

Jug's Club: A Prohibitionist's Worst Nightmare

The central hub of activity and welcoming watering hole after a hard day in the woods—whether a regular workday, one shortened by low humidity, or an unrelenting rain—was Jug's Club.

The tavern set on Central Avenue, the main thoroughfare through Sutherlin, and adjacent to the one and only bank, which occupied the corner. Entering town from the south on Highway 99 and making a right turn put you on Central Avenue. Central and old Highway 99 were one and the same for a block; then at the corner where the bank stood, Highway 99 veered off to the left and wound on northward.

Not only the busiest bar in town, Jug's held the reputation as the most heavily patronized business. It served as the primary social club and recreational center for the loggers and a number of mill workers during the long and ofttimes lonely winters. It became the acknowledged hangout for these hard-working, hard-drinking men to congregate—some during the day, some during the evening, and others establishing a continuity between the two shifts. It was the chosen spot to celebrate birthdays, holidays, a good-sized paycheck (or the prospect of one), or whatever other happy occasion should arise.

Moreover, the mourning of sorrowful events took place there, with no shortage of persons willing to take on the role of sympathetic, impromptu grief counselor—not only commiserating with the dejected, but unselfishly joining and abetting in the drowning of tears.

Much unsolicited marriage counseling transpired inside these walls, any number of which counseling sessions terminated in the law office of Gerald Kabler, conveniently located just upstairs and to the left.

All in all, Jug's embodied the 1900s hatchet-wielding prohibitionist Carrie Nation's worst nightmare!

If everyone in town worked hard, they played with equal vigor. What a person considers afterhours play or amusement is a matter of individual taste, but in Sutherlin it almost certainly centered around some manner of consuming varied multiple alcoholic beverages—either as a singular pursuit or combined with other diverse activities.

"Temperance" and "moderation" were not words that come to mind in describing the lifestyle of the loggers who frequented Jug's, or, for that matter, in depicting the lifestyle of the majority of the town's citizenry as well.

Inside Jug's the majority of zealously pursued activities were advertised games, such as billiards and pool. The bar's slogan, "Do Your Logging at Jug's" (or "Bud's" when it changed hands) held more truth than fiction, as B.S.ing was the most finely tuned and highly participated-in pastime. But depending on its legal status at any particular time, the game of choice was gambling — the unadvertised indulgence.

A second saloon, known as the Pastime, awaited carousers on the opposite side of the street towards the west end of the block. A slightly more genteel establishment, it held itself up to be the gathering place for the less boisterous townspeople and businessmen. Here an eager, love-struck logger felt free to invite a lady friend for the evening. Not only did they serve food, but the atmosphere was more conducive to audible conversation and the discreet whispering of sweet nothings in the ear.

As Forrest Hollandsworth, the logging superintendent at Weyerhaeuser, recalled: "… to go out to dinner or anything like that, generally you'd go clear to Roseburg. That was about the nearest place. Sutherlin was, of course, a small town, but about the only place you could get anything to eat there was at the booze joint, beer joint."

That is not to say that the free-spending loggers didn't shell out money at the Pastime, only that this tavern was talked of as the more respectable of the two. Compared to Jug's, the Pastime looked like an oasis of peace and tranquillity.

At First Sight

The building housing Jug's Club had more depth than width. The front of the red brick building began at the sidewalk on Central Avenue and ended in a dark, narrow, and littered dirt alleyway in the back. On either side of the entrance were two plate glass windows.

Pulling open the heavy wooden door and stepping inside, you found a solid hardwood bar standing about three steps off to your right. At that end of the bar it took a turn and jogged in towards and butted up against the back wall, which was a common wall with the bank. This side area afforded sufficient space for three or four patrons to agilely maneuver around that corner and be seated.

The front bar ran about halfway down the depth of the room and could seat 15 comfortably, and 20 if squeezed in. It retained its old original brass railings. At an earlier point in its service, dirty manure-specked cowboy boots rested on the brass foot rail, but now its dulled and marred surface supported the weight of dusty, weatherbeaten work boots and the much maligned caulks.

Several feet beyond the end of the bar a concocted high barrier rose upward. This tossed-up structure separated the back bar, the bar itself, and the bar stools from the pool tables spaced around the back of the tavern. The wooden shield's intended purpose was to prevent any misshot wayward cue ball from errantly ricocheting off a back pool table and zapping an already dazed and befuddled imbiber seated at the bar.

Between the end of the bar and this partition Jug made allowance for an aisle. It measured wide enough so the bartender and service people could carry in case after case of beer for unloading into the refrigerated back bar.

The mirrored backbar held the glasses, ash trays, and various advertising displays and paraphernalia that constituted the tavern's decor.

Located up against the wall adjacent to the back bar stood a heavy, thick-walled and ornately decorated walk-in safe that reached almost to the ceiling. At any given time, this safe harbored thousands of dollars earned directly or indirectly from the lumber industry. Money, like the beer, flowed freely, and good business sense dictated keeping plenty of currency on hand to cash payroll checks and bankroll the gambling activities. Considering the whopping amount of money on the premises at any one time, it was amazing that Jug's Club never experienced a holdup.

Positioned on the opposite side of the room were highbacked wooden booths where buddies could comfortably convene to do a little logging over their Olies. Depending on the current legal status of gambling (explained later), on a moment's notice these booths might be removed and replaced by the more profitable green-felt poker tables.

Tickled with his find, the tavern owner took the time to polish old salvaged brass spitoons and scatter them conveniently about the floor. This accommodation filled the bill for those thirsty adept souls who'd mastered the delicate art of chewing a wad of Copenhagen while at the same time sipping a cold one.

Without giving much thought to proper placement or scale, several titillating girlie calendars depicting scantily clad ladies were thoughtfully tacked up here and there on the walls. This not only spruced up the place but more than likely adorned the walls for the patrons' convenience. After all, the calendars conveyed the express message that knowing what day it was was half the battle.

Mending Fences

A waist-high railing resembling a picket fence ran the width of the tavern dividing it in half. The fence reached from the far wall of the booth area to the service aisle. This sectioned off the tavern into separate activity areas. An opening centered in the railing permitted even the most unsteady customer to grope his way to the back to use the rest room, play pool, or watch a poker game.

Gracing the place with its splendor and basking in the knowledge that it was the loveliest object on the premises, was the colorful, glitzy and never-silent jukebox. It claimed its rightful place of honor butted up against the picketed partition near the bar.

Behind the waist-high barrier sat the pool tables and a snooker table. More poker tables were strategically spotted around the back room so as to keep the card players out of the line of jabbing pool cues. Seated there any time of day or night, sober-faced men jealously guarded their staggered stacks of poker chips while intently studying the fanned-out cards in their hands.

Although sturdily constructed, the picketed divider had seen hard times and suffered through more than its share of chaotic scuffles. Replacing and resetting pickets seemed to be an ongoing process. Finally, no longer able to withstand the pounding and beating it took when 200-pound men, sent reeling from a well-placed punch, slammed against it or groggily staggered into it, the inadequate battle-worn fence came down permanently.

Locking Horns at Jug's

Jug's on a Friday or Saturday night boiled with electrically charged energy, and the robust, bawdy (mostly male) patrons were crammed in toward the bar with standing room only, sometimes three deep.

It definitely was not a place for a lone woman or several female friends to gravitate in search of a leisurely drink, that is unless they hoped for a bit of quick action. They'd be guaranteed of finding it there.

As might be expected, fights were a fairly common, although unprogrammed, occurrence. The majority of loggers frequenting the place came for the camaraderie—to play cards, shoot pool, or just to kill time.

Yet, put together a mix of vigorous, virile, and jostling men who have consumed copious amounts of beer over a short period of time, with little more than salty beer nuts to dilute the alcohol's effects. Then add a smattering of short tempers fueled by the tension of long winter months with hit-and-miss work and the resultant money problems; augment with quick fists acquired from a background of resolving matters and frustrations in this manner, and you have the recipe for a minor discord to end up in allout fisticuffs.

This combination, bolstered by the fact that, for the most part, this establishment was devoid of women—and thereby any feminine prodding to, "Leave well enough alone," or just plain, "Let's leave!"— added to the volatile ingredients. It set the stage for a petty squabble or argument to swiftly magnify into a good old-fashioned barroom brawl.

Invariably the bully bad guy, fortified by booze and a bad temper, lurked on the scene ready to bristle at the wrong word or any misconstrued sideways glance; or the broody one wearing a perpetual chip on his shoulder who never lacked for someone willing to take a crack at knocking it off. On top of that, the usual ongoing unresolved rivalries endured, and it only took a spark to reignite an old trivial feud.

Much the same as words and the cleverness to combine and turn them to his advantage are an articulate lawyer's weapon in settling a dispute—and the means by which he earns his living—so too were a logger's hands, quick wits, agility and strength his tools. Not only were they the means by which he put bread on the table, but the most logical tools of choice to iron out differences. Either one's ability to turn his best attributes to his advantage enabled him to resolve a dispute and determine the outcome of an argument. In either case, guilt or innocence, right or wrong didn't matter. What did matter were quick wits and ability. To think any differently was unrealistic.

Furthermore, it must be recognized that Jug's patrons (or for that matter, the Pastime's) were mostly young to middle-aged men. Few more mature, mellowed-out men were on hand to act as level-headed arbitrators in an effort to avert the tensions and persuade angry young men to simmer down.

That is not to say the joint was devoid of peacemakers, but their effectiveness hinged on their proximity to the argument; their ability to get an iron grip on one of the protagonists and hold him back, and another handy to grab his struggling opponent and escort him outside for a cooling-off period.

If a peacekeeping mission failed, or one of the combatant's friends thought an arbitrator a little too rough on his buddy and jumped in with a few punches of his own, it had the potential of erupting into a free-for-all.

At any one time, it was a draw of the cards as to the mix of temperaments present in the patrons, or the number of cool heads vs hot heads. As a rule, though, Jug's held a happy jumble of patrons.

Put Another Nickel In

Walking past Jug's any time of the day or night, the melancholy and plaintive refrains of classic country melodies such as Eddy Arnold's "It's a Sin," Patty Page's "The Tennessee Waltz," or Hank Williams' "Cold, Cold Heart" could be heard filtering out through the walls. A quarter in the colorful ornate jukebox, its bubbling columns of liquid encircling the front, bought you six songs. And about the only time the 78s weren't spinning on the turntable was when the machine begrudgingly broke down or was irreparably broken up.

As the hour grew later and the beer consumption greater, the atmosphere grew proportionately noisier and rowdier. So the old Wurlitzer's volume would of necessity be adjusted upward. By late evening, the whirlpool of sounds culminated in an ear-shattering, high-decibel pitch. This blare amplified to the point that the sound waves ricocheted off the walls, vibrating and rattling the plate glass windows.

If the nickel deposited in the jukebox paid off with a jazzy ragtime or toe-tapping rhythm such as "Muskrat Ramble" or "Alexander's Ragtime Band," the noise level inside ascended to a deafening volume. Capturing the mood, those windows appeared to visibly pulsate to the beat of the music.

The selection made by the logger coaxing his nickel into the slot of the red, yellow, and orange glowing illuminated box set the tone and provided a clue to his immediate mood. Mostly vocals emphasizing broken hearts, failed promises and undying love, the songs functioned as background music while sipping suds or shooting the bull.

Follow the Bouncing Ball

At one point during that era the most worn and repeatedly punched button on the jukebox was the one that chose the popular high energy tune, "Deep in the Heart of Texas." This song was guaranteed to make the rafters vibrate and bring the house to its knees, begging for mercy. With a four-four beat, it called for a slight bit of high-spirited audience involvement. This active participation came in the form of vigorous clapping four times at the appropriate short break in the tune. This rest came right before the phrase "deep in the heart of Texas," which lyrics were to be sung in unison with the recording artist. The pause occurred routinely after every second stanza.

A catchy and infectious tune, it bordered on being a compulsion to clap and unreservedly shout/sing "Deep in the Heart of Texas" where intended.

A choir director couldn't have asked for a more animated and enthusiastic group than the boys at Jug's. Failing to fully grasp the subtleties of hand-clapping and clearly hindered by their involvement in other activities, when the brief pause in the song signaled them to clap, they cleverly improvised.

JUKE BOX
The style of the Juke box that was in Jug's Club.

Those encumbered by a spread of cards in their hands, or the grasp on a beer bottle while observing a game of Nineball, plainly suffered under a handicap. Gallant and not lacking in resourcefulness, however, they rose to the occasion by vigorously stomping their heavyweight boots four times in unison on the beer-splattered wood floor; then bellowing out their memorized lyrics.

Meanwhile, not to be left out, any patient pool player leaning on his cue stick while awaiting his turn to shoot, banged his cue stick on the floor in lieu of clapping. Having a vested interest in breaking his opponent's concentration, the louder he could thump the cue stick the better.

Those merriment seekers hammering down a few while wedged in at the bar, their heavy scuffed boots propped on the brass footrest, were prohibited from this style of stomping accompaniment. Although a tall order, with a touch of genius they adroitly circumvented this obstacle. They joined in with their fellow performers by pounding their gnarly fists on the bar and, like worldclass performers in harmony with the rest of the choir, belting out at the top of their lungs "Deep in the Heart of Texas."

If, when their cue came, one hand firmly gripped a beer bottle, they pounded both the open bottle and their free fist on the counter, causing any beer glasses or bottles to levitate several inches down the bar.

In their daring role as backup singers, this gifted and energetic cast of performers with their rhythmic improvisations were above reproach. They quite literally had the ability to bring the house down.

But, alas, the old jukebox' days were numbered. After one particularly fierce rough-and-tumble skirmish wherein several combatants took turns being slammed into the old Wurlitzer, its glowing bubbling lights were punched out. Its fate sealed, the gurgling life's blood slowly oozed from its ruptured columns.

Being dislodged from its groove on the spinning record, the needle scratched shrilly across the surface causing the 78's melody to abort. As the remaining stack of records dropped down helter-skelter, the refrains of "Mockingbird Hill," "Rag Time Cowboy Joe," and "Goodnight Irene" all interfused into a medley of babbling gibberish.

Workmen later hauled away the demolished jukebox to make room for an equally glitzy new model. Playing it safe this time, the new purveyor of tunes was placed back away from the bar and up against the far wall near the booth area. This relocation pretended to keep it out of harms' way and upped its uneven odds for survival.

Nonetheless, leaving nothing to fate, this replacement was enshrined in a custom designed wooden box. This shroud covered both its vulnerable sides and front, thereby protecting it from shameful wear and tear for which it was ill-prepared.

The designer of the custom made box crafted an opening in the front just above the jukebox's lower illuminated columns. This permitted an undaunted customer to deposit his money and push the white plastic buttons to make his favorite selections. The carpenter also hung a hinged door in the front providing for easy access to the cash box and occasional maintenance.

A Stranger Blows into Town

Traveling from the north in his light green Mercury, the rumpled tourist had pushed his car hard all morning. An unusually warm and muggy day, he'd driven with his windows down most of the way. The heat gauge's fluctuating needle had him sweating it out even more. Slowing for a corner, a metal sign informed him that he'd hit the town of Sutherlin. Hot, tired, and thirsty, he couldn't wait to stretch his legs and get a cold frosty one.

Seeing the welcoming signpost brought to mind the talk he'd heard about this town—in particular the reputed announcement made by

Walter Winchell on a recent evening newscast. Walter Winchell was the famous news columnist and radio broadcaster who introduced every broadcast with "Good Evening Ladies and Gentlemen and All the Ships at Sea." Rumor had it that Mr. Winchell reported something to the effect that the residents of the small logging community of Sutherlin, Oregon, consume more alcoholic beverages per capita than any other town in the nation.

Whether there was any truth to it or not didn't matter, and word circulated around town like wildfire. Receiving national recognition was nothing to sneeze at, and—no matter what the cost—the loyal patrons of Jug's set about upholding this well-earned notoriety.

"Well," he thought, "I'm sure there'll be no problem finding something to drink here."

Pulling up in front of the tavern and parking, the beer sign lettered on the window caught his eye and lured the unsuspecting gentleman into Jug's.

Nattily dressed for the weather, he wore his new seersucker Palm Beach suit. In hopes of catching any breeze that might come his way, he'd left the top couple of buttons of his wrinkled checkered shirt undone. White ventilated shoes adorned his feet as he walked to the door of the tavern.

Opening the door, he stepped inside. And right away he wished he'd peeked in before he walked in.

Feeling more than a little out of place after assessing the patrons, he hastened to order a beer from the bar. Paying up, he grabbed the icy cold beer and headed for one of the booths off to his left, away from the loud banter of the men at the bar. Their quizzical glance as he walked in told him he stuck out like a sore thumb, and he wanted to steer clear of that crowd.

After sliding into a booth, he wished he could blend into the woodwork. But winter white registered quite a contrast to the booths' dark wood. He surveyed the tavern on the sly and tried to dispel his uneasiness. Humming softly to himself, he drifted along with the "Tumbling Tumbleweed," the mournful prairie lament wailing from the jukebox. He gave thanks for the whirling revolving fans suspended from the ceiling. They at least circulated the blue smoke-filled air and created a pleasant breeze directly above him.

Fidgety, he toyed with the cold bottle, twirling its damp bottom on the table's surface. He noted the crudely carved words scratched into the wood, "Kilroy Was Here." Well, what the hell, he hadn't expected the Copa Cabana or the Stork Club!

Almost finished with his beer, he had to admit it sure hit the spot despite the circumstances. Wrestling with the decision whether to stay and have a second or cut out, his eyes were drawn to a young, broad-shouldered logger bellying up to the bar.

Without giving it any thought, he glanced at the logger's back. His attire appeared no different from the rest of the patrons: a pair of jeans, a drab plaid shirt with broad suspenders, and dusty down-at-the-heels boots. Something tugged at his curiosity and caused him to steal a second glance. The back of the logger's faded jeans showed more wear than the front, and, oddly enough, one pant leg sported a neatly sewn patch behind the knee.

Baffled, he pondered the logger's jeans.

The backside of the young man's pants at the thighs and calves were darn-near threadbare. He reasoned that even if you sat on your butt all day, it would be damn hard to wear out a pair of denim pants on the backside, especially the back of the knees.

Not able to account for it, he wondered what kind of work the guy did.

In the process of mulling all this over, the mystery grew. A darkblue line ran across the top of both pant legs just below his slender, muscular derriere. The seat of the pants wasn't nearly as worn as the pant legs.

Still perplexed, he decided to forego that second beer and hit the road. Digging into his pockets for the car keys, he watched as the young man suddenly turned from the bar and made his way towards the back room. Now he noticed the same strange darkblue line running around the top front of the jeans, just below the crotch. The front legs of the pants showed little wear.

Putting all that aside, it was time for him to get out of there before some more roughnecks appeared on the scene.

Easing his way to the door and heaving a sigh of relief, he shoved it open and emerged into the bright sunlight.

What the visitor didn't know, but continued to puzzle over as he watched the town fade in his rearview mirror, was that the strange handiwork on the pants was an example of frugal loggers recycling their work pants. Plodding through the thick underbrush with its sharp snags and snapping branches; pulling wire rope and dragging lines back and forth across the front of a pair of pants; or being down on your knees most of the day setting chokers, soon wore through a pair of new jeans. A thrifty housewife, who in like manner turned collars so as to salvage a shirt, would cut her husband's jeans off near the crotch, turn the pant legs around and then sew them back on, thereby doubling their wear.

Anyway, he was happy to be out of there. He knew one thing for sure. No thirst or hankering for a brew could ever again coax him back into that hell hole, thank you!

CHAPTER NINE

Now I Lay Me Down To Sleep

Across the street from the bank building and Jug's sat the once stately Sutherlin Hotel, a two-story brick building constructed in the early 1900s.

It was a large and grand hotel for Sutherlin's size. Depending upon the whims of management, anywhere from 42 to 46 rooms awaited tuckered-out guests. Except for several on the ground floor, most of the accommodations filled the space on the second floor. One bathroom did duty for two rooms.

These quarters, though cramped and sparsely furnished, were adequate. Heat for each cubicle radiated from hot water radiators; air conditioning came by fits and starts. The amount of stagnant air taken out and the amount of fresh air vented in depended on how wide the occupant threw open his window and the direction of the prevailing breeze.

The rooms on the hotel's east side overlooked a good sized balcony bordered by a waist-high, white banister. This balcony jutting out from the side of the hotel functioned as the roof over several shops and a portion of the restaurant downstairs. None of the rooms offered what might even remotely be called a scenic view.

The Fruit Fiasco

After the hostelry's construction, these lodgings primarily rented out to travel-weary prospective investors who arrived from the Mid-West, many via train. They came from as far away as St. Paul, Minnesota, making their journey in a private pullman car owned and operated by Luse Land and Development Company, Ltd. of Sutherlin and St. Paul. These travelers suffered the long journey expecting to purchase land from Luse Land and Development Company—that is, if the hype checked out.

This land scheme involved dividing the valley into ten and twenty-

SUTHERLIN HOTEL
Constructed in 1914 after Sutherlin Inn
burned down. Photograph circa 1920.
Photo courtesy of the Douglas County Museum
of History and Natural History.

acre fruit tracts. Adequate water for irrigating the orchards would be supplied by a gravity irrigation system This development company vigorously promoted sale of these tracts by placing ads in numerous publications, which touted the fruit-growing climate and livability of the Sutherlin area.

In an interview of Maurice Vogelpohl, a resident since 1910, given to Jim Bendt for a Sutherlin High School history project, Mr. Vogelpohl colorfully depicted this land rush.

"They set up in the Sutherlin Hotel on account of the homey conditions. They was traveling men. Most of them in those days came by horse and buggy or by train, had to wait for train connections to leave." The niceties included a bell hop who toted your bags to your room. Temporary workers signing in on the hotel's register, rented their lodgings at a reduced monthly rate.

LUSE LAND AND DEVELOPMENT
Prospective buyers arriving in pullman car from the east to scout out Luse Land and Development orchard plots. Photograph circa 1909. Photograph courtesy of Bud and Vera Holm.

Ten and Twenty Acre Orchard Homes
(*Left*) Page from November 1909 *Better Fruit Magazine* advertising orchard plots in Sutherlin Valley. Compliments of Bud and Vera Holm.

But the grandiose land project didn't work out. One local historian says its demise came about because the land was unsuitable for fruit growing. Other sources say it failed because of the growers' inability to market and ship the fruit. Whatever the reason, many of the investors suffered tremendous losses, some losing their life savings and going bankrupt. A number of diehards, hanging on by the skin of their teeth, stayed in the area—later facing the onslaught of hard times caused by the Depression.

J. F. Luse, the president of Luse Land and Development, who made his home in Sutherlin, also ended up broke and is reputed to have committed suicide.

The Worse for Wear

Not in their wildest dreams could the forefathers have foreseen what misfortune and changing times would bring to their grand edifice.

This lovely Grande Dame of the early 1900s had evolved into the bag lady of the 1940s. Its shabby rooms were now rented out at weekly or monthly rates to single, footloose loggers and family men forced to leave their families behind. Like the single men, the husbands and fathers came to Sutherlin to work. As soon as they could find anything resembling permanent housing–any shack would do—they would send for their wives and kids. In the meantime they called the hotel home.

For a few unfortunate, desperate teachers, it solved the problem of where to lay their heads. As unappealing as it was, it was a godsend.

Fronting on main street, on either side of the hotel, was a barber shop on one side and a beauty shop on the other. A large porch ran across the front of the hotel between the shops. From the porch you walked through the double doors into the generous lobby.

Despite her fading beauty, the lobby hung on to some semblance of its former elegance. Complete with over-stuffed chairs and couches for lounging, it remained quite plush and comfortable.

A huge brick fireplace centered in the lobby's east wall added to the hospitable atmosphere. Day and night during the winter, a cheerful crackling fire burned in its firebox, warming those relaxing and shooting the breeze.

Walking straight on through the lobby towards the back of the hotel, the smell of coffee brewing pointed the way to the coffee shop. The main entrance to the restaurant was through the door on the east side. Customers seated at the counter or in the booths along the wall had their choice of breakfast, lunch, or dinner.

Besides a convenience for the resident loggers, the restaurant provided a place for the bleary-eyed travelers arriving via the Greyhound bus to grab a quick bite. The Greyhound Bus Depot sign posted outside the hotel advised that this was the point of entry to, or departure from, Sutherlin. How this news sat with you depended on how your fortunes were running.

Lettered on the lobby's front window was the ever-present admonition "No Hobnails." This legible warning always afforded me a quiet grin. It conjured up visions of a headstrong, grimy logger, who couldn't be bothered with most admonishments, wearily trudging in after a miserable day in the woods. Begrudgingly halting on the porch, he bent over to begin the tedious task of unlacing and removing his grimy caulk boots before entering the lobby. Then, shoulders slouched, he grasped the tops of his dirty boots and daintily tiptoed through the lobby and up the stairs—all the while fretting about a visible hole in his sock.

When work was slow, a certainty in the winter, playing pool, cards, or just chewing the fat over at Jugs—anything to break the bleak monotony—was far better than lingering around a lonely, dismal hotel room.

Whatever our current source of prostitutes, a little lustful dalliance provided a brief but pleasant diversion in an otherwise long day. Could you request room service for a pick-me-up quickie? Well, of course!

CHAPTER TEN

Sex, Gambling, and the Law

Gambling in Oregon was illegal. Yet, back in the 1940s it flourished. As a teenager, I knew gambling was a major pastime and source of recreation for a good part of Sutherlin's male population. It was a fact of life much the same as prostitution. At least this I'd seen with my own eyes. Mistakenly sticking my head inside the wrong door, I caught sight of players slouched over a poker table with chips stacked in front of them. They weren't playing penny ante!

Indeed, while working for Jerry Kabler, on those occasions when he departed the office without apprising me of his destination, I suspected that more than likely he could be found downstairs in Jug's playing poker. But, I knew enough to keep my mouth shut.

The simple truth is I came by this knowledge via his clients. Oft times after informing a client that I didn't know of Mr. Kabler's whereabouts, I'd be told, "I bet I do. Two-bits says he's down in Jugs playing poker." With this, hot on the trail, the stalker made a beeline for the door. Depending on the importance of the business and, no doubt, how Jerry's luck was running, Mr. Kabler would show up back in the office along with his client.

Certainly, if gambling was illegal, the town's only attorney wouldn't openly sit downstairs at a poker table studying his hand over a stack of poker chips.

The Oregon Penal Code declared gambling illegal, but the law ran counter to the facts.

Beating the Bushes

In doing research for this book, the inconsistencies first needed to be unraveled. I knew it was a tall order and wouldn't be easy. It proved to be downright frustrating.

My search began by seeking out oldtimers who would have been at least 21 years old in the late 1940s. I found that the grim reaper had been making his rounds of the youthfully challenged and collecting his dues.

As one seasoned attorney told me, "Time flies. Anyone who would know about gambling, etc. in Douglas County so long ago would be in a cemetery."

Be that as it may, I managed to dig up a few.

Those old chaps only added to the confusion. Each recounted stories to substantiate why he believed wagering was legal or why he knew it was illegal. Without batting an eye, some said gambling was permitted—that they openly played in full view of anyone coming on the premises.

Others said it was in violation of the law and they played secretly. A few oldsters told of clandestine games set up and run in empty houses; others related exciting stories about raids carried out by the State Police.

For the Record

Bill Kenwisher, a proud septuagenarian, talked about gambling.

"I used to think nothing of betting $50.00 on a game of pinochle. Played with Ed Smith a lot—wasn't illegal as far as I knew. We gambled at Jug's, Pastime and the barber shop by the appliance store.

"Herb Hogan ran the cardroom in back of the taxi office. There would be no money on the table—had to get chips from the banker [who held the money] and then cashed them in. Played pinochle in the area where the pool tables were [in Jug's.]"

The secret here was if law enforcement didn't see any cash on the table or money exchanging hands, they were precluded from making any arrests.

Dwayne Linton, a resident of Sutherlin for 50 years, remembers Jug Allen, the owner of Jug's, sitting at a table with his back to the wall, acting as banker.

"You bought your chips from him, and he took his cut," as all bankers did.

After Jug Allen sold Jug's to Bill Montgomery, he continued operating under the same name.

Then all of a sudden, gambling was forbidden. Dwayne recalled the State Police bursting in and zealously making arrests and confiscating the gambling devices.

Questioned about gambling, Dave Pichett, a dedicated and hardworking police officer in Sutherlin for 26 years, and high on the list of respected citizens, stated, "Herb Hogan used to run and organize games. Had arthritis, couldn't do much of anything else. The houseman took a rake off. There was also someone named Louie, an Italian, kind of dark, who ran games. Can't remember his last name.

"I've seen bets of $50.00 on a game of pool in Jugs, and the pinball machines paid off. George Master ran a poker game in the back of the taxi office. Sometimes the State Police and Sheriff's Department would come in and make a few arrests and confiscate the equipment, but they'd be back in business the following week."

As Dave mentioned, even the innocuous playful pinball machines in Jugs paid off.

By today's standards, the wager of $50.00 on a friendly game of pool or a hand of pinochle seems like pretty high stakes — one heck of a lot of money, especially for those earning it by the sweat of their brow. But to put the amounts wagered into its proper perspective consider that, according to the U.S. Bureau of Labor Statistics' CPI, $50 in 1949 translates into $350—give or take a few bucks—today.

Upstairs above Jug's were living quarters. When not occupied for that purpose, or for all I know maybe when it was, rumor had it that super-high-stakes poker games took place. Dave Pichette stated that because this constituted private property, the odds of anyone being busted were practically nil.

Taking into account the relatively large amounts wagered in full view downstairs, there is little reason to doubt the stories of high-stakes games upstairs. Access to these exclusive games was guarded and limited to the high rollers known to carry large wads of cash.

✳   ✳   ✳

As an aside and by way of a little intrigue, Dave's reference to an Italian by the name of Louie jolted my memory. I recalled the surname. Italian names in Sutherlin were as rare as frog's hair, except for the Nicolazzi family. And it took all us Okies, Arkies, Swedes and Krautheads quite awhile to learn to pronounce that.

Sometime in 1948 a new girl, about 15 or 16, appeared at school. She was small in stature with short dark hair, and her name was June.

As a rule, newly arrived students, adopted the attitude that, like it or not, they were stuck in Sutherlin to stay. They hastened to demonstrate an openness that invited new friendships. But June presented an air of aloofness that implied, "Keep your distance and don't ask any questions." Her walk and deportment communicated, "I'm hard as nails and nothing you say or do can hurt me."

Although she courted no friendships, most of us made every effort to be friendly. As it so happened, June turned out to be a great softball player. Getting involved in sports seemed to loosen her up somewhat, even to the point that she managed to beam a halfway smile every so often.

Her demeanor indicated she'd been firmly lectured along the lines of, "Don't get too friendly and don't answer any questions. We may not be here that long anyway."

Later on, in an attempt to get on a more favorable footing, I inquired where her Dad worked. Her reply, "Jug's." Her terse response signified the end of conversation. I either heard or surmised that no mother was around.

Several times I saw her appear out of the alley from behind Jug's headed for school. I couldn't imagine where she lived, as the only structure in the alley was an old shed behind Jug's, and it appeared too small to be habitable. But then people scrambled to find any sort of living facility. Not wanting to embarrass her, I never asked.

Since Dave's reference to Louie with the Italian last name, I've wondered if maybe she lived upstairs above Jug's partitioned off from the boisterous poker games. Kids have lived in worse arrangements.

As mysteriously as she appeared, she disappeared with no goodbyes.

The Ins and Outs of the Law

After the passage of so many years, I began to get the sinking feeling that I was looking for the proverbial needle in the haystack. But by lucky happenstance, I was put in touch with a knower-of-all-things-past, at least as it related to Douglas County's recent past.

James McGinty, an attorney, was able to shed light on the puzzling gambling yoyo of long ago. Mr. McGinty, right up until 1991, continued to practice law and live in Myrtle Creek, a small town about 20 miles south of Roseburg.

In his role as City Attorney for Myrtle Creek for 26 years, encompassing the years 1948 to 1974, what he hadn't seen, he knew about. Early on in this position, his duties included drawing up legal contracts between the town and its taverns. These contracts stipulated how and when a monthly "table tax" of $100 per table would be paid to the city.

What it all boiled down to was that the law forbidding gambling was one that local governments conveniently ignored upon finding it too costly to enforce. "Too costly" meant it caused a significant loss of revenue to the bars, taverns, and private clubs, all of which, in turn, fed money into the county coffers and the county's rebel towns. In Douglas County, where willy-nilly enforcement held sway, gambling came and went strictly by the fickle finger of local politics and politicians.

Left to their own devices, each town enacted its own rules. Not surprisingly, the enactment of ordinances permitting gambling involved some exchange of money to the city. It also trickled down to line the pockets and grease the palms of a few county notables.

Many of the small towns in Douglas County such as Riddle, Myrtle Creek, Canyonville and Sutherlin, all within close proximity to the county seat, levied this tax on each gaming hall or saloon. The going rate seemed to be $100 per month for each card table on the premises. As Mr. McGinty stated, "The tavern owners were tickled pink to pay this 'tax.'"

During the 1940s these tables generated more revenue for the cities than from any other taxable source.

Go to Jail: Do Not Pass Go

The law prohibiting gambling provided that all persons arrested for operating, playing, dealing, or otherwise being involved in any gambling activities for value, "will be guilty of a misdemeanor, and upon conviction thereof will be punished by a fine of not more than $500, and will be imprisoned in the county jail until such fine and costs are paid...." OCLA 1939–49 Article 5 of the Penal Code, 132.

The law further provided, "and all such fines and forfeitures, except costs, shall be paid into the county treasury, and constitute a part of the school fund."

Ironically, and not going unnoticed at the time, education and schools benefited from the illegal gambling activities.

The Poor Loser Law

Going on with his explanation of gambling, Mr. McGinty referenced another law on the books whereby an agitated loser could recover *double the money* lost gambling.

The law specified that this double value could be recovered, "from the dealer or player winning the same, or proprietor for whose benefit such game was played or dealt...." OCLA 1939–49, Civil Code, Sect. 64–102.

But, Mr. McGinty explained that, "ordinarily, it was not the men who complained of their losses, but their wives."

It stood to reason that the disgruntled gambler had no desire to lodge a complaint, or threaten to file suit, since, more often than not, he was thereafter routinely barred from again placing a wager at that establishment. As word circulated, he found himself unwelcome in other gaming houses.

As an attorney, McGinty explained how he handled the matter whenever an irate wife stomped into his office shrilly complaining about the money her husband blew at a specific gaming house. He'd casually pick up the phone and call the offending establishment. After stating his business, he advised the proprietor that it would be wise to just return the money her husband lost. This headed off the filing of a formal complaint for double the money.

As a point of interest, and representative of the times, it should be noted that if a complaint was formally filed to recover double damages, the law stipulated that should the defendant being served be absent from the home when the serving officer arrived, the server could make substitute service on any member of the household over fourteen years of age, provided that person was white. This statute was repealed about 30 years ago.

The Spark Arrester

Inasmuch as the rise and fall of the indulgent vices was determined by the leanings of the District Attorney in office, the decline of gambling and prostitution within Douglas County can be traced to the election of a bright, energetic, down-on-all-vices District Attorney. Robert

Davis swept into office in 1949. As James McGinty declared, "When Davis became D.A. is when prostitution and gambling were in trouble. Prior to that everything was pretty lax."

But it was incredulous to believe that those who retained an ardent penchant for gambling and enjoyed the camaraderie of playing cards for hours on end, and the pleasurable adrenaline rush of a winning hand, would easily accept now being told, "You just can't do that anymore!"

Bewildered and angered by the sudden change, they thought of it as a raw deal and an infringement on their rights. These free-spirited, willful, and indulgent men believed this irksome turnabout, instituted with malice, would certainly cause them serious psychological damage.

Just because some jugheaded District Attorney decided to flaunt his authority only meant that immediate innovative action was imperative.

Resolving not to buckle under to tyranny, the gaming establishments and the gamblers who frequented them were hell-bent in their resolve to circumvent this sudden whimsical enforcement. Thus, the birth of the rooms behind the taxi office, the barber shop by the appliance store, and the other hideaways.

Yeah, All Men and Everything Illegal

Written historical interviews from the Douglas County Museum offer a clear picture of the righteous Robert Davis butting heads with those determined to play by a different set of rules. His zealous attempt to put a damper on and destroy the happy times of the gamblers, took out loggers, lawyers, and respectable businessmen alike. In these interviews, all references seem to be A.D. or B.D. (After Davis or Before Davis.)

R. J. Duffy, a restaurateur, worked as a bartender at the Veterans Club in Roseburg. Off and on, he'd also worked as a bartender and cook at other establishments in the Roseburg area. In his interview for the Douglas County Museum on June 21, 1978, he responded to questions about gambling and smokers in Roseburg, and particularly at the Veterans Club,

Q: Smokers?

A: Yeah, all men and everything illegal, crap games and so forth. I ran the poker game, and I would see someone losing money and I would win some and give it to them and pretty soon we were raided and we were all in jail. Exciting times, but it was part of growing up.

Q: What kind of stakes did they play for?

A: Table stakes. We played for what you had on the table, in other words we had no limit.

Q: What was the most you ever saw someone win or lose?

A: Oh boy, I personally have made a bet of two thousand dollars.

Q: Did you win it?

A: It wasn't called. I've seen winners go up to six thousand dollars in a game...

Duffy also described the sign posted above the bar of the Veterans Club that read: "This is not a combat area," which would indicate that not all of their customers were well behaved. He did add, "We had some pretty good swingers up there."

In continuing with his interview, Duffy went on to talk about the Highway 99 Club. Now, despite my tender years, this was something about which I had personal knowledge.

This roadhouse, called Club 99, was situated about half way between Sutherlin and Roseburg, six miles south of Sutherlin to be exact. It advertised familystyle meals.

Club 99 also had a bar where an at-least-21-year-old boyfriend of any one of us girls could leave a bottle in residence behind the bar. On two occasions, fresh out of high school and accompanied by the guys, a few of us stopped by Club 99 after a movie. The only appeal was forbidden fruit: the challenge to see if we girls could get away with ordering a drink from the bar. On neither occasion did it present a problem.

Decked out in bobby socks and saddle shoes, I made no attempt to appear older than my 17 years. I don't believe I could have pulled it off even if I'd made the effort. Obviously, we weren't too concerned about the consequences of flaunting the law.

On one occasion, about five of us were sitting around a table sipping our drinks when a waitress came scurrying over and whispered in an urgent tone, "If any of you are under 21, you'd better leave. The law is on its way out." Someone in law enforcement was on the take.

Naturally, we departed posthaste.

Q: Tell me again what happened at the 99 Club?

A: It was a slow night and there were a few of the fellows that wanted a game. I was cutting the game, and all of a sudden they were stomping on the roof and pounding at the door. All hell broke loose. There were 17 State policemen and the District Attorney, Mr. Davis, the crusader. I lost my chips and the rack and everything there....

Q: The D. A. at that time was Mr. Davis?

A: Bob Davis was a very smart person and politics was his goal. If you spit in the street, Bob was there, and he broke me and the others. Bob went on to the Legislature....

Q: Could you explain how the payoff system worked?

A: It seemed like in Oregon that there was one man who ran one area. I was acquainted with the one in Portland and the one in Bend. Mr. Howard Kerr, he was the one that was close to the District Attorney, and the only one that the District Attorney would talk to. He would gather up from all the people that were gambling and take his little cut, and he would then split that with the District Attorney.

Q: Did you have to pay him monthly?

A: Well, if there was a big game going on, he was right there. I don't know how he ever knew but he was always there.

Q: How much did you have to pay him?

A: It varied. Around 15%.

Q: The District Attorney at this time wasn't Davis, was it?

A: I think it was Carter. He did real well on District Attorney's pay. He wound up with a big trailer court out here, and that sort of thing.

Q: When Davis came in, was there a sudden change or a gradual change?

A: Well, the word was out and we just shrugged our shoulders....Nobody could touch Bob. I'm not going to mention names. After all this was over with, another man was District Attorney and he is now one of our presiding judges, and he was having an affair with my hustle partner's wife. He met with me one time and we had a piece of cantaloupe and coffee and he wanted to know how much he could get if he opened an account and so forth and so forth, but I was such a coward, I wouldn't take it, so nothing ever happened. I decided that was enough nonsense and I went straight. I put my mind in frying pans and such, which was the best thing that ever happened to me.

Asked what card games were most commonly played, Duffy replied that the popular games were stud, draw, and low ball. He maintained he could have made a living playing poker.

As an afterthought he commented, "This is funny, you think you're so smart. I was playing blackjack out at Kennedy's [Dutch Mill] one night and I broke a guy and he was an Electrolux salesman, and before the night was over, I had one of his vacuum [sic] cleaners and when he came out the next day to deliver it, he sold me more attachments to it than I wanted, so I don't know if I came out ahead or not."

And the Bottle Went Along

In Oregon, up until the mid 1950s, the sale of hard liquor over the bar was prohibited. If you wanted to spend time drinking socially in a restaurant or bar licensed to dispense hard liquor, you had to provide your own bottle of booze.

A bottle of liquor could only be purchased from a state-owned liquor store, which required you to have an Oregon Liquor License. This license was issued to anyone 21 years of age or over, after the payment of one dollar. The license was good for one year.

You then took your bottle to the establishment you wanted to frequent and gave it to the bartender; he tagged it and placed it on a shelf behind the bar. When you requested a drink, the bartender poured from your bottle, added the specified mix, and then charged you for the mix and service.

If you were a real socializer frequenting different taverns, this meant an investment in several bottles of hooch spread around several barrooms. If you couldn't afford the cost of that, then when you left the joint where you'd been whooping it up, your bottle accompanied you on home, or it tagged along to your next destination.

Going back to Duffy's interview, a question arose about an earlier remark he'd made concerning bootlegged whiskey.

Q: You mentioned that you bootlegged whiskey and that was in the forties and fifties. I didn't think that was around at that time?

A: I meant that we sold it illegally. Up until May of 1953, you couldn't buy a drink over the bar. You had to go to the liquor store and buy it, then bring it with you. They [bartender or hostess] gave you a number and plastered it on the bottle so you would know that it was your bottle. It was carried into the bartender, then you ordered drinks out of your own bottle.

Q: Then did you pay the bartender?

A: Oh, yes, you paid 15 to 25 cents a drink, just for the ice and service. Then there was always somebody that couldn't make it to the liquor store or more people showed up and the booze went too fast. So we did sell it over the counter but there were many people that did the same thing. In fact, they all did. It was called the house bottle.

Q. Was that ever cracked down on?

A. Oh, yes, one time I was cooking over at Melody Inn and my partner was tending bar. Some people came in. Somehow he sold them a drink out of the house bottle and this guy had a little syringe that he sucked some up into and he used it for evidence. We got a 30-day suspension for it.

Good Gals in the Wrong Business

Prostitution, like gambling, flourished during the period B.D. But my knowledge of the emporium of sin in Sutherlin and Ruth's El Rancho at Wilbur had all been acquired by hand-over-mouth gossip and whispered teenage revelations.

I wanted to validate the location of those bordellos. And the way to do this was at the same time I interviewed oldtimers and time-worn loggers about gambling. After they told me what they remembered about that subject, I'd introduce the topic of prostitution. Not surprisingly, everyone appeared rather puzzled regarding this subject, except for Sutherlin's surviving police officers.

But in shrugging their shoulders, no less than three or four different persons told me, "If you want to know about any houses, you should talk to old so-and-so." (He'll remain anonymous, but I can conjure up his image as a young logger.) As an aside, each person referencing him also mentioned, "But, he's so damn deaf, he probably couldn't understand you anyway!"

Considering the frequency Amorous Anonymous' name popped up, he'd acquired quite a claim to fame in his endeavor to sample all the wares. From the awe this gentleman generated for his obvious stamina, fervent ardor, and zealous patronage of the pleasure palaces, it could be deduced that he quite unwittingly screwed himself to deaf.

Albert Flegal owned and operated a business in Roseburg known as Flegal Transfer and Storage Company. He advertised "all kinds of hauling, moving, packing, and storage." He became Roseburg's mayor, later a Douglas County Commissioner, and served as State Representative and State Senator.

A portion of his interview given to the Douglas County Museum on March 27, 1978, as it relates to prostitution, follows.

Q: Who carried most of the clout, was it the political figures out front or was there some silent ones in the background?

A: I think there were a lot of people who thought that they were powerful, but they weren't. I don't recollect anyone that was pushing at me. I remember one lawyer in town that is now dead asked me if I would approve of another house of ill fame. He said it would be worth $800 a month to me. I insisted that it had to be paid to me in some country that had no extradition and it had to be at least a million dollars. So that deal dropped. I've had women come over to the Flegal Transfer office wanting to start a house of ill fame in Roseburg and lots of times guys have come over and offered me a price on diamond rings if I would let them open a house. I remember one time I called Kennerly, Chief of Police, and I appointed him Chief of Police, and I said, 'Chief, there is a man sitting here

and he has offered me some rings wrapped in toilet paper if I let him open a house of ill fame in the house across from the Rose Hotel. I just want you to know if he opens it that there is going to be a new Chief of Police.' 'Sure, Mayor, it will never open.' And this other gal came in and gave me a song and dance about opening a house and I just told her that it couldn't be done, Davis was District Attorney...."

Q: I'm interested in these houses of ill fame.

A: You never heard of them before?

Q: Oh, yes, but were they in Roseburg?

A: ...The Family Hotel which was about a block from the Rose Hotel and that was run by Ruth, and Mary ran the other one. Mary's house was on a circuit and they traveled from town to town. This was a big white house and it had a big circular driveway around to the back, so prominent business men could get in to see them without anyone else seeing them. But all I had to drive in those days was a yellow pickup with Flegal Transfer on it. When Mary would call and ask me to come down and pick up some things for her girls, in those days the S.P. had a train, and take them to the depot, their trunks and suitcases and so forth, well, I always went myself and I would always drive up to the back door and I wouldn't knock. I would just go right on in. Mary always sat in a chaise lounge with her back to the door, and she had this one girl who was almost deaf and I didn't know it, and as I walked in this girl jumped up and walked toward me saying something, and Mary said, 'Oh, no, that is the Mayor.' But they were here for a long time. Mary finally moved out by the Highway Department to a house out there and then she no, first she moved out by the Green bridge out by Dillard. Then she moved up by the Highway Department and she died there. All the relatives that didn't want anything to do with her when she was alive were down here the next day to pick out the things that they would inherit. Mary was a good gal and a good friend. But she was in the wrong business, but that was her business.

A Lady Named Fern

James McGinty, thinking back to gambling and prostitution B.D., and Robert Davis' A.D. campaign to clean up the county, articulately refreshed his memory in writing. Although his references are to Myrtle Creek specifically, his first-hand account could pass for most of Douglas County during that era.

> I came to Myrtle Creek in February of 1948. There was at that time a plywood plant and saw mill in Myrtle Creek which employed around 700 men. The streets in Myrtle Creek were largely gravel and dusty. Many people lived in tents. The city was like a boom town.
>
> There were, I believe, two taverns in Myrtle Creek when I arrived. One was owned and operated by Kenny. In addition to the sale of beer, his establishment had three or four card tables. All of the tables were open to unlimited gambling. The owner or house took a percentage of each game. The games were heavily patronized…
>
> The city at this time usually taxed the owner of the gambling tables $100 per table per month. The tavern owners were tickled pink to pay this tax. In fact, a former city recorder of Myrtle Creek made the owners of the taverns build a new jail to house trouble makers. Gambling and drinking caused lots of fights…
>
> Myrtle Creek also had a brothel just outside the city limits run by a lady named Fern. There was in the city a taxi that took the clients up the hill to Fern's establishment. The owner of one of the taverns later married Fern and made her a righteous woman. The end of the brothel came after one disgruntled client arrived there about 4:00 a.m. He was told that the place was closed, he threatened to kick the door in if they didn't admit him, he received a bullet in his foot for his trouble. The place shut down soon afterward.
>
> The District Attorney of Douglas County in office at this time was very lax and easy-going. He made no attempt to stop the gambling or prostitution. Slot machines were openly played at the Elks Club in Roseburg and many other places.

> In the year 1949, a new lawyer named Robert Davis, decided to run for district attorney. His platform was based on the premise of no gambling, slot machines or prostitution. The tavern owners tried to get other attorneys to run for district attorney on the platform of an open city. Gerald Kabler and others ran as a candidate for the job. Mr. Kabler and the others were defeated by Robert Davis, who campaigned on his stated platform. Davis won by a wide margin. All gambling, slot machines and prostitution came to a halt. Shortly thereafter the police raided the [exclusive] Elks Club in Roseburg and confiscated all slot machines.

Nevertheless, the fat lady hadn't finished her song. Mr. Davis had about extinguished the fires, but the embers continued to smolder when he up and resigned in 1952.

Not quite enough time had passed, however, for the memories of the good times to have burned out. Nor had the small towns' thirst been quenched for the easy money that flowed into city coffers. The tavern owners and many of the city fathers believed that with a little ember stoking they could rekindle and revisit the vices.

This caught the already battle-weary Sutherlin Police Department in a crossfire, resulting in an outright tug-a-war.

CHAPTER ELEVEN

"So Many Police Chiefs Ago"

At the height of Sutherlin's heyday, law and order was chaotic at best. The turn over of its police officers, not to mention police chiefs, occurred with predictable regularity.

Not by any stretch of the imagination could the town be considered dangerous, nor were ordinary citizens terrorized. The average resident would have been hard-pressed to find a safer place to live and raise a family.

A young girl could walk home late at night from a movie or visiting a friend without fearing for her safety. I don't recall even the rumor of a rape committed by any of the men. For the most part, violent crime was nonexistent.

In reality, the loggers kept to their own rules of conduct and peevishly resisted being told what to do, when to do it, or in what manner. In no way did they exhibit what might be construed as hardcore criminal behavior, rather their folly lay in having a penchant for pleasurable wrongdoing and an inclination toward unruly behavior. They blithely violated what they perceived as half-baked laws that made no sense anyway, and looked upon these violations as victimless minor infractions—nobody really got hurt.

Yet, for them, a defined although invisible line existed that was not to be stepped over. For example, their rules of etiquette censored using foul language around ladies, and they were quick to admonish anyone who forgot the niceties. As police officer Audie Campbell (1954–1957) acknowledged, "They were all good guys, just liked to fight and drink."

Maybe a little rough around the edges, on the whole they were honorable, hard-working men. Many were family men, who gave no thought to hitting the bars until Friday or Saturday night. And as sole bread-winner, it wasn't open for discussion with the little woman.

On their night out these men showed up at one of the taverns to play cards, shoot the breeze, and maybe tie one on. Although not looking for trouble, should it find them, they were up for it.

Also in their midst were the unpolished rogues who mulled about at all hours pursuing their common excesses in the bars, and this tended to band them together in a fringe fraternity. Within this brotherhood existed a few bad eggs habitually looking for trouble and ready to fight, and they seldom failed to be generously rewarded.

The Light at the End of the Street

The lion's share of police calls to require immediate assistance originated from fights in progress. If a group of bemused onlookers hadn't yet gathered, it might be permitted to play out on the street, and the unrulies let off with a verbal reprimand. Nevertheless, within the confines of a business it did tend to be somewhat disruptive to other customers. And besides, if allowed to continue it acted as a magnet, sucking in others just hankering to poke someone—anyone. Kinda like an itch beggin' for a scratch—they just hadda do it!

An officer's response time to a call for help was determined by what crime-in-progress held his attention at that moment. If the sole officer on duty was tied up and not patrolling the street, it might be awhile.

During the day the call rang in City Hall, and if the officer was away from his desk someone else answered the ring. Across the street from the present City Hall, and on down towards the end of the main street, a red light sat atop a pole. This beacon lit up the moment the phone rang. If an emergency generated the call, the red light remained on. Otherwise, the answering employee took a message and switched it off. When outdoors, the officer kept an eagle eye on that pole, and the instant he glimpsed the signal, he either headed for his office or called in.

After hours when City Hall closed, an incoming call triggered the red light. The caller, knowing the next course of action, hung up, waited five minutes, and called back. If all was well, this allowed the officer sufficient time to hustle back to the police department to catch the call. Prior to implementing this response system, a notice ran in the local paper, and notices were posted and circulated around town informing people how it operated. If it was a serious emergency, the caller could call the Roseburg Police and they could radio the Sutherlin police officer. If he was patrolling in his car, this made the response time a little quicker.

Down the line as funds became available, a phone was installed in a lock box up the street about a block and a half from City Hall. This made response time quicker and easier. If the officer was patrolling in the vicinity of the boxed ringing phone, he could answer it himself. Or if he missed the call and the signal light glowed, he could hang around that phone for the five-minute repeat call.

Soon afterwards, a white globe replaced the red one, as a white light would be more visible from a distance, especially at night and when pouring rain drenched the skies.

The Three Terrible Transgressions

Fights in progress routinely led to arrests for disorderly conduct. Then handcuffed, the unrepentant were escorted over to the city jail for a cooling off period. For all they knew, they just might get to savor a slumber party in the slammer.

For the officer, curbing skirmishes involved more than abating disorderly conduct, it often meant being drawn into the thick of things where holding your own was the best you could hope for. An officer getting clobbered by a flying fist escalated the charge to the more serious offense of resisting arrest.

Besides disorderly conduct, Officer Dave Pichette identified two other reasons for spending the night in Sutherlin's pokey. One was defrauding an innkeeper.

"Sometimes there were three or four at a time in jail for not paying their hotel bill."

And the other law broken with regularity was the antiquated law prohibiting lewd cohabitation. Again, victimless little infractions, and, "Hell, no one got hurt."

The law prohibiting lewd cohabitation, Book 3, OCLA (1940–1955) Sec. 23–903 stated: "If any man and woman, not being married to each other, shall lewdly or lasciviously cohabit or associate together, such man or woman, upon conviction thereof, shall be punished by imprisonment in the county jail not less than one nor more than six months, or by fine not less than $50 nor more than $300."

James McGinty explained that the punishment and/or fine was meted out by court order. While serving as City Attorney of Myrtle Creek, he recalled the filing of only two cases.

"Both involved women and they each served three or four days in jail." (Authors' note: Did I miss something here?)

Being picked up and booked on any of these three charges, respectively evoked logical responses of: "Well, he just pissed me off, and if he got hurt, that's his fault. The bastard deserved it, He shouldn't 've been such a smart ass in the first place." Or, "Hey, he started it!"

"Well, yeah, I beat the guy out of his rent money, but I couldn't help it. I'd've paid him if I'd had it—lost my last 60 bucks playin' poker." Or, "If I could've got more than a half-day's work in last week. The damn weather caused it. What the hell, the guy wasn't hurt, I didn't strong-arm him. You can't get blood out of a turnip, ya know."

Lewd acts? "Jackass law anyway. Hell, I ain't no goddamned priest, and she sure as shit ain't no nun!"

All in a Day's Work

As sure as the sun peeked up over the Cascades each day, somewhere within town at least one of the police could expect to have his authority challenged, and if he blew hot and cold or backed down, he was perceived as weak and ineffective. The loggers had a nose for timidity and could smell it like a dog sniffs out a fox. It was a cat-and-mouse game they enjoyed playing with each new hire, and they chose not to take on the role of mouse!

Losing face caused many a rookie to hand in his badge. As James McGinty stated, "It wasn't dangerous work, it was frustrating."

For the rookie it verged on being downright humiliating. Gaining respect came by way of earning it. It wasn't awarded with the badge.

After strapping on his gun, should a new officer display the slightest inclination toward cockiness or a yearning to flex a little muscle, he was barking up the wrong tree. And big didn't account for much either, as bigger and tougher boys sat swilling beer in Jug's.

Pulling a gun on a stiff-necked logger because he didn't jump when ordered would prove a dumb move. It just wasn't done. If he should walk into that hornet's nest and the subsequent uproar, his best bet was to leave town under cover of darkness.

As retired Chief Richard Crumal (1953–1971) exclaimed, "The loggers showed no respect for the law." Affirmed in different wording, McGinty stated, "They thumbed their noses at it!"

Move Over, Big Bad John

No past reflections by the Sutherlin Police are complete without mention of the Parazoo boys.

Among Sutherlin's loggers, far and away the toughest of the lot and infamously known to police chiefs for over 20 years, were the Parazoo brothers, particularly Doug and Shannon. Legendary for being big and bad, it didn't take much to yank their chain.

"The Parazoo boys—there were four of them—were tough," exclaimed Crumal. Actually, there were six boys, but four stuck in Crumal's mind.

The Parazoo family descended from several of the original French-Canadian settlers in Oregon, and their lineage traced back to Chief Concommly of the Native Chinook Indians.

With few privileges, theirs was a poor but proud family of nine children. Born in a log cabin built by his father, Brad, the fifth child, served with honor during the War. Wounded in battle on Okinawa he received the Purple Heart. He also participated in the liberation of the Philippines. There was no room for whiners and criers in that family, and they were known to be hard workers.

Holding the reputation as the man you didn't want to come up against was Doug Parazoo. Tangling with him was like walking into a buzz saw.

"Doug was really tough and caused a lot of trouble—just plain mean," Crumall noted.

Doug and Shannon Parazoo were inclined to act out, as we say of children. They loved nothing better than a good fight.

Carla, one of Doug's daughters, doesn't recall her dad being mean, just the opposite—she remembers him as a "sweetheart." As a child at home she saw the softer side of him.

Born in 1921, Doug, like so many kids from that era, came up the hard way. Always big for his age, he went to work in the woods when he was 12 years old. Before that, he attended the Fair Oaks School, which was five miles from town, through the fifth grade. How the everyday blatant discrimination he was subjected to at school affected him can only be surmised. It would seem that the source of drinking water for the pupils was the old water pail and communal dipper. Carla recalls her dad candidly telling her he wasn't allowed to drink from the same dipper as the other children because "he was an Indian."

DOUG PARAZOO AND BROTHER SHANNON
Photograph taken in 1967. The boys were a little older, but no smaller. Sister, Opal, on the right. The younger generation referred to them as "The Big Three."
Photograph courtesy of Carla Inda, daughter of Doug Parazoo.

Carla said it was hammered into them as children that they must treat everyone the same, and if they put down or ridiculed anyone they got into big trouble. Doug minced no words in warning them that they were not to tease or make fun of anyone.

✳   ✳   ✳

Dave Pichette, Sutherlin's seasoned police officer, began his career in Sutherlin in 1947, and during his tenure worked under ten different police chiefs, most of it on the night shift.

"Week nights I patrolled alone, but on weekends there were two of us on duty."

He described Sutherlin's jail at the old City Hall as consisting of, "two cells and a bullpen, a big room for exercising. Sometimes seven or eight in jail at one time. Nothing to have three, four or five in there sleeping."

Not a particularly tall man, Dave had a stocky build and carried himself tall. Affable, goodhumored, and blessed with common sense, he enjoyed the high regard of the loggers and townsfolk alike.

"A sense of humor was never lost in the situations I found myself in."

Responding to a call about a fight at Jug's, and many times on duty by himself, Dave reminisced, "I took people out of there fighting. The place would be so packed you could hardly get in. Always went in by myself as I worked by myself."

If quick scrutiny revealed the situation out of control, and no backup stood in the wings, he knew he would be hard put to handle it by himself. Keeping his fingers crossed that a Parazoo wasn't at the center of the melee, he still held an ace up his sleeve. Squinting through the tavern's haze, he pinned his hopes on spotting and then catching the eye of at least one Parazoo. Two would be great, but one pretty well evened the odds.

Elbowing their way towards each other until they came within hearing range, Dave unceremoniously hastened to deputize Parazoo. Now, in a flash any needed reinforcement was at the ready and poised to strike.

Conscription of one of the Parazoo boys for deputy duty wasn't that unusual. Logic decreed that if you're going to have trouble, you want what could spell double trouble on your side. Sutherlin's veteran cops all agreed they couldn't wish for a more gungho, better equipped deputy.

For the Parazoos, hearts leaping with joy, they felt as though they'd been given a pass to tread on enchanted ground. Handed to them on a silver platter was the right and authority to indulge in activities that usually got them in deep doodoo: grabbing other tough guys, jerking and smacking 'em around to make them do what they said and if they didn't, they got to slug 'em. And all the while breathing freely as these blessings bestowed upon them by the wave of a wand were legally ordained by law. It didn't get much better than that!

Crumal tells about the time he was summoned to a domestic disturbance involving Doug.

"When I got there, I told him to calm down and quit fightin' with his woman. Doug asked me, 'And who do you think's goin' to make me?' I replied that 'I was!' With that, Doug hauled off and hit me in the face and broke my glasses. Then I hit him with my billy club across the forehead and the blood started to spurt and roll.

"I got Doug's attention and that seemed to be the end of it. I put him under arrest and hauled him off. While he was being held, someone asked me if I was gonna take him to the hospital, and I said 'Hell, no, let him die—he tried to kill me!'" After that incident, Crumal renamed his billy club his "Doug Club."

"When I needed it, I'd say, 'Where's my Doug Club?'"

**POLICE CHIEF
RICHARD CRUMMAL**
Chief of Police 1953–1971.
(Deceased)

No Turkey Trots at Turkey Hall

For all his years on the force, Dave Pichette admitted to a one-time injury in the line of duty. This took place in 1952 and, as it so happened, didn't occur in Sutherlin, nor did it involve a logger.

After responding to a call for assistance from Turk Manning, Oakland's chief of police, he was assaulted.

"[Also], I was following up on someone on probation and got jumped. Bunch of kids. Got my leg broke."

He also suffered head injuries and later required an operation to reset two broken bones in the leg.

Turk Manning, feeling much like the Maytag Repairman during the week, held the position of Oakland's Chief of Police for 15 years, back when the town had a staggering population of around 800 hardy citizens. Except for a few stores, a bank, and City Hall, the town didn't consist of much. A tavern sat on the corner of the main street and Old Highway 99, and that tavern along with the Saturday night dance, were the major source of the town's problems. Outside of this wing-ding, with the exception of the residents, no one found much occasion to venture there.

The dance was held in what was known as Turkey Hall, an old corrugated-tin building taking up half a block right off the main street. It was a much-looked-forward-to weekly event for many of the older teenagers (at least those whose parents remained in the dark as to the attendant hell-raising), a few of the more exuberant county residents, loggers on the prowl or loggers who just plain loved to dance.

No wallflowers sat wilting on the benches as the inexhaustible dancing loggers were undeterred by sprained ankles or wrenched knees. Should any pain resurface, it was anesthetized during intermission. Self-prescribed pain killer was dispensed from the flea market of alcoholic beverages available from most vehicles parked outside. The upraised car trunks identified the dispensing stations. Here a fellow could get a shot of anything from gin and Seven to Four Roses. A cold beer, specially iced for the event in a metal tub covered with a dampened gunny sack, might be what the doctor ordered.

If prior to intermission, pain threatened to slow them down, there was no reason to suffer, as relief was just a stone's throw away.

Not swamped with police work during his tenure as police chief, Turk likewise held the titles of constable, dog catcher, and deputy sheriff. And still not cracking under the strain, he found himself charged with grading the streets, park maintenance, and ringing the old school bell that signaled the ten o'clock curfew.

With his own hands, Turk built the town's city hall, fire hall, police station and jail receiving no extra compensation for his efforts.

But Saturday night was payback time for the peace and quiet he'd enjoyed all week. When fights erupted in or outside the dance, it was Turk who turned into a caricature of Dirty Harry and walked unaccompanied into the thick of things. He was known as "a no-nonsense cop. Turk didn't fool around." For the most part, when the chips were down, or he found himself in tight places he dealt with it by himself.

Who's the Baddest of Them All?

Another logger with a reputation guaranteed to send shivers up a rookie cop's spine and cause his stomach to convulse into rubbery knots was the logger known locally as Montana.

Dode Winter, the Weyerhaeuser truck driver, related a story about Montana that I found a little hard to swallow.

It seems that Dode was killing time shooting pool in Jug's one evening when Montana ruffled someone's feathers. He was on hand to see Montana arrested, then handcuffed, and whisked outside to the sidewalk. For some reason he didn't understand, a group of onlookers tagged along. Figuring they must know something that he didn't, he followed the followers outside.

"I couldn't believe what I saw. Montana, quick as a flash, jerked his wrists apart and snapped the handcuffs. I never saw anything like that in my life. He was one tough sonofabitch."

Thinking this an exaggeration that time likely cultivates, I wrote it off as an old memory grown bigger than life. Sometimes memories inked into the far reaches of our minds become smudged by time. I feared repeating something so farfetched would be discrediting. No one would believe it anyway.

But, lo and behold, in 1993, after meeting with then Chief Richard Schwartz, the same story popped up. Damn, it was true. Not even Paul Bunyan received accolades for anything like that! Yet, admittedly, Paul Bunyan never found himself in handcuffs.

Richard Schwartz, Police Chief of Sutherlin from 1987 to the end of 1993, signed on with the department in 1965. I hoped to find out from our arranged meeting if he knew why Sutherlin was unable to retain five different police chiefs over a specific one-year period during the fifties. Although before his time, he'd been on the force long enough to hear all the old stories and rumors that made good conversation. And a copy of an old newspaper article posing the same question was on display in the police station.

"I really don't know," was his reply.

While reminiscing, he abruptly broke off in mid sentence. Out of the blue, he inquired if I'd ever heard of the Parazoo boys? It became apparent that the Parazoos were legendary, and like all the veteran police officers, no review of the past was complete without their mention.

My answer proved irrelevant since the eagerness in his voice implied, "Hold onto your hat, you're about to hear a couple of unbelievable true stories!"

As he began to speak, the awe in his voice and the excited twinkle in his eye gave away his concealed admiration for flesh and blood men who possessed all the idiosyncrasies and performed the amazing feats from which folklore spring.

"Montana, I think his first name was Jake, and Doug Parazoo were the only men I've ever seen that could stand flatfooted while shackled in handcuffs and with a jerk, snap them in two."

Chief Schwartz further explained, "Handcuffs are made to swivel purposely at each end so they [the connecting chain] can't be snapped by a twisting rotation of both hands."

Schwartz's still-handsome face grinned as he told the next incredulous tale on the tip of his tongue.

It seems the police received a call that Doug was creating a disturbance at Jug's. Where else? Responding, Schwartz parked the patrol car directly across the street from the tavern, and dispatched his fledgling to deal with Doug. He waited alone in the car. For all he knew, Doug might be feeling a little out of sorts today, and this could be worth the price of admission.

The young officer, with one hand on his billy club, and seeking to hit upon a gait somewhere between a swagger and scared stiff, swung into action on his determined mission: to apprehend and take into custody the devilish errant Doug Parazoo.

And, like a boy waiting with delighted anticipation for his Dad to plop down on a planted whoopie cushion, Schwartz couldn't help but chuckle to himself. A few minutes later, his wait was rewarded. The door to Jug's swung open and out marched the proud rookie, shoving the manacled Doug through the door head of him.

Once outside, Schwartz said, "Doug, true to form, disgustedly fixed the officer with a withering stare, expelled a giant grunt, yanked his arms apart, and snapped the cuffs," as though they were linked by rotten cotton rope.

Remembering the look on the stunned officer's face, he broke out in laughter.

"His face turned white, his eyes got wide, and his jaw dropped in disbelief."

The Targeted Prey

When the occasion arose to hire a new city cop, it wasn't unusual for the initial recruitment to take place off the streets. If the quarry looked large enough to handle the job, he was approached. Following this first contact came the formal interview.

In March of 1953, Richard Crumal, recently retired from his position as police chief of Portersville, California, was on his way to Alaska where a job awaited him.

"I stopped over in Sutherlin, and there was no chief and I was asked to stay a few days. After three days as a patrolman, I inquired as to when I was gettin' paid? They informed me that they were considerin' me for the job of chief. City had given me five days to work. I stayed on, then became chief."

Crumal reflecting on his career, pointed out, "Sutherlin was tough, but I came from a tough area and knew I could handle it. The loggers showed no respect for the law, but I felt I knew how to do it. Get their respect; otherwise you wouldn't last long because they challenged you all the time."

In the Crumal vs. Parazoo confrontation, his attention-grabbing blow to Doug's head, administered via the Doug club, fed his reputation for standing his ground and gained him the sought-after respect of the loggers.

Audie Campbell was another such mustered officer. But this time, Crumal did the stalking.

Audie, a large man with a round, pleasant face and a quick winning smile, looked every inch the Arkansas farm boy he was.

Fresh out of the service following a tour of duty in the Korean War, he received a letter from his sister living in Sutherlin expounding on all the work available there. He arrived in Sutherlin Thanksgiving night of 1954, only to find that he couldn't buy a job—at least not in the dead of winter.

"When I first got here I thought this was the most goddamned ugly town I'd ever seen. Figured I'd find work and get outta here back to Arkansas in a year. But within a year I liked it and stayed. Been here over 40 years."

Several days after his arrival, sporting a red shirt and bib overalls, he sauntered into the police department to pick up a driver's license application. After requesting the form, he waited by the counter. His Arkie accent plus his husky size drew Chief Crumal's attention. Crumal arose from behind his desk and moseyed over to strike up a conversation with the unsuspecting candidate.

"Hi, I'm Chief Crumal. Where ya from in Arkansas?"

Surprised, Audie answered him, then asked, "How'd ya' know I'm from Arkansas?"

Crumal explained that he recognized the accent because he'd lived in a town not far from there.

The truth was that Sutherlin had become a melting pot of Southern accents. A discerning ear could pick out the Okie from the Arkie, and the Texan from the Okie or the Arkie. Almost no one admitted to hailing from Missouri.

When queried, "Where ya from?" They'd take their pick of other southern states to tell their little white lie, but never admit to Missouri. Whatever the reason, at least in their eyes, being a native of "The Show Me State" lowered their status to the very bottom of the heap.

POLICE CHIEF WALTER "TURK" MANNING
Chief of Police in Oakland, Oregon from 1952–1967. At the time of this book's publishing, Turk was 95 years old.

Next, Crumal asked, "Have ya ever done any police work?"

Audie replied, "Nope, never have."

"You look like you're big enough to handle the job. I have a man talking about quitting in a few days. Would you be willing to give it a try?"

"I'd take 'bout anything. I need a job."

Music to Crumal's ears he'd nabbed his man! Sliding a job application over to Audie, the chief inquired as to where he was hanging his hat. Audie gave him directions to his sister's house, then went about filling out the application.

His hopes renewed, Audie handed Crumal his completed application, bid the chief a polite "see y'all later," and wandered out into the drizzling rain.

"Three days later he came'n got me, and asked, 'Are ya ready to go to work?'"

One last-minute, non-negotiable condition of his employment was that he damn-well better like to fight.

Crumal told him, "These loggers, they like to fight. If you don't like to fight you might as well head on down the road."

Audie's face lit up as he exclaimed, "Hey, you sure's hell got the right man 'cause I love to fight!"

Puzzled, I repeated the words. "You love to fight??"

Audie's eyes sparkled as he replied, "Yeah, I love to fight—have since I was a kid!"

I said I couldn't understand that. Nobody likes to get hurt.

Patiently, Audie explained, "At the time it doesn't hurt—the adrenalin's agoin'. Sure maybe next day it hurts some, but you're young and it don't bother ya much. I love it!"

The combination of adrenalin and testosterone must equal something that constitutes an adrenasterone high?

Audie remained on the force for three years, more than sufficient time to learn about the bawdy house near the old football field (now the City Park). I'd done such a good job of keeping my mouth shut upon learning about it back in the late forties, that now I couldn't find anyone to confirm its existence. But Audie did.

"It was near the old Chenoweth place, east of the city park on Everett Street, off Umatilla. It burned down years ago."

After signing on with the police department, he heard about the earlier State Police's investigation of Chief Bingham and the circulating rumors that he and a local businessman owned and operated the fun palace.

"The State Police were set to pull off a raid, but for some reason, the raid didn't work out." Thus Bob Bingham's overnight departure.

Another theory regarding Bob's tail-between-his-legs exit from stage came from Dave Pichette.

Dave stated that he (the Chief) was messing around with someone else's wife.

"This was the woman he got tangled up with, and the Mayor fired him. I didn't know about Bingham being investigated for running the cat house, but I wouldn't be surprised. Perhaps his getting fired over the woman was just a cover-up for what he was really doing and why he really got fired."

Whatever the reason, apparently the duties of police chief failed to occupy enough of his time.

✳   ✳   ✳

Police Chief Schwartz was another officer subtly pressed into service. In 1965 he applied for an opening in the fire department. He passed the examination with flying colors. But prior to going on the payroll, the department head thought the strapping young man better suited for police work.

"He said he thought I wanted to be a police officer."

Having no previous experience at either job, he went along with the draft, and obtained his training on the street.

No further stories were forthcoming as to other police chiefs or rookies plucked off the street or conscripted by the power of persuasion. But with the town's turnover of peace officers, there probably were others. They just passed through the revolving door so fast they can't be remembered.

The Crow Bar Hotel and Guests

"The Crow Bar Hotel" was a term coined by the entertaining and eccentric character Elso Sunshine Silver to identify the city jail. Called Sunshine, he was adopted as the town clown, which role he gladly assumed. Like so many others, where he hailed from is unknown, but you could swear some of these characters floated in on a magic carpet.

Audie Campbell thought back to the time he saw Sunshine heading for a roundup, trotting down the street and swinging a lasso.

"Sunshine, what the hell ya' doin'?" Audie shouted.

His response, "There's a goddamn cow loose in town an' I'm gonna lasso the sonofabitch."

"Get the hell outta the street!"

"I gotta catch her. She's a bullin'."

Audie warned, "If ya don't get outta the goddamned street, I'm goin' to lasso *you* an' take *you* to the Crowbar Hotel."

Amongst his recollections of guests registered at The Crow Bar, Audie particularly called to mind a Christmas party where he felt as though he'd been drawn into the eye of a hurricane. The impromptu, last-minute invitations extended to the State Police and all Douglas County law enforcement signaled the cessation of festivities.

Ed Funderburk, besides being a successful logger and contractor in town, was additionally noted for his parties. Now this wasn't because of the attendant elegance or the beautifully set table where his finest silver and crystal goblets were set out. Rather, those attending knew they were in for a hell of a night and the beer and other intoxicants flowed freely.

Regarding Funderburk's parties, Pichette was quick to point out, "There were always fights and trouble."

Audie went on, "He had a Christmas party and invited all his employees. Looked like everyone in town worked for him by the size of the party.

"We got a call there was a fight. Went up there and broke up the fight between two guys. One took a swing at me and hit me on the ear, so, I took a big five-cell flashlight and hit him with it. I said 'Okay you sonofabitch,' and slammed him into the police car, then I threw him into a cell [at the jail.] Already had one drunk in that cell and, come to find out, it was this guy's brother-in-law and they hated each other's guts."

Audie knew he was out on a limb and needed to call for backup—the night was still young.

Since they covered the beat on the cheap, calling for help necessitated returning to the police department. As Audie explained it, their car radio wasn't exactly state-of-the-art even for that time. They could receive, but couldn't send. At least not any distance.

Therefore, Audie had to hustle back to the office and telephone the State Police and the Sheriff's office in Roseburg. Then Roseburg called or radioed sheriff deputies stationed in the outlying towns to respond to Sutherlin's emergency.

While Audie was engaged in calling for help, the newly arrived jailee found his bladder about to be overwhelmed by the high volume of beer he'd consumed.

The cell consisted of two bunks and a commode. But instead of availing himself of the commode placed on the east wall he, perhaps mistakenly and perhaps not, began to divest himself of his beer in an area on the west wall where his brother-in-law lay sleeping it off.

While holding for the State Police, Audie heard a commotion in the cell.

Springing to his feet, he barreled back to see what was going on. He arrived just in time to observe the peed-upon leap off his bunk, screaming, "You sonofabitch, you've been pissin' on me long enough and you're not gonna to do it anymore!"

With that, another fight was on. Audie settled this by separating them and locking the new arrival in another cell.

Audie continued, "It was a helluva night! We went back to Funderburk's party, knowin' there were still 50 to 100 people there. By then two more fights were goin' on.

"At that time there were only seven deputies in the county and they were all at different places like Glide, Elkton, Reedsport. Douglas County's a large county. They finally got the party stopped when the deputies and the State Police stormed in." (It is worth noting that many of these deputies had to speed in from as far as 60 miles away to arrive at Sutherlin.)

"God, those were fun days!"

Bringing up the subject of Doug Parazoo and Montana, Audie expounded on Montana.

"The man had big hands and big wrists. The handcuffs barely fit over his wrists."

Holding up his beefy hands, Audie said, "His fingers were twice as big as mine. He had massive hands."

"But, there was one fellow I knew, a logger who lived in Oakland, his wrists were so large the handcuffs wouldn't fit!

"But, before I tell you 'bout that, do you wanna know how those two guys broke their cuffs?"

With that Audie demonstrated how it was done, repeating the demonstration until I had it down pat.

First it is important to note that the connecting chain attached to the inside of each handcuff was made out of steel, not stainless steel as the newer cuffs are.

In tests performed on the newer cuffs, Chief Schwartz said it had been calculated that you'd have to exert about a thousand pounds of pressure to break the chain. Audie felt that with the earlier steel chain it probably required between 500 and 750 pounds of pressure to snap the chain. And these two fellows could do it!

The chain connecting the two cuffs is about one-and-a-half inches long. With a person's cuffed hands either hanging down or extended in front of him, there is insufficient allowance for even an extremely strong man to attain ample leverage to snap the chain.

But Doug Parazoo and Montana had massive muscular wrists and a trick up their sleeves. With hands placed together in front of them as though in prayer, each hand was tightened into a fist. This butted the fists up against each other with the middle knuckles of each hand touching or almost touching, depending on the tautness of the chain down at the wrists.

They were now ready to use the mechanical advantage of the crowbar and fulcrum, the crowbar being their wrists and arms, and the tightened fists the fulcrum. A fulcrum is described as "the support on which a lever turns in raising or moving something."

In one swift strong yank the wrists were pulled outward and upward. As the opposing fists pushed against each other they provided the additional force needed to complete the pull upward and break the chain. At the instant the chain snapped, for that one split second the top knuckles of each hand would touch as they hit together.

Although others begged to be shown how to do it, they were powerless to pull it off.

✳   ✳   ✳

Now, back to the hulk of a man with the cuff-proof wrists.

"He got drunk in Sutherlin and I tried to arrest him. We got into a scuffle so I wrestled him down into the gutter. His head was up against the curb. His head was turned to the side and I had my knee on his neck. I threatened to put more pressure on his neck if he continued to fight. I was right in the middle of him with my knee against the side of his throat.

"Then I went to cuff him, but the cuffs wouldn't go 'round his wrists. I couldn't believe it! I told him, 'You son-of-a-bitch, you're gonna get up from here and walk straight ahead of me 'til we get to the jail.'

"We had two blocks to walk. Told him I'd shoot him if he made any funny moves."

Inquiring as to whether he meant what he said, Audie responded, "You're damn right I would've." Probably in the leg I figured, then just drag him on up the street.

No one would have taken too much note.

The Curious Case of the Churning Chiefs

The rowdy fun times were inching to an end. Yet the colorful characters remained on the scene, gradually fading away and being swallowed up by the transitional times. Nevertheless, none went down without a fight. This is evidenced by the rapid turnover of Sutherlin's police chiefs.

During the one-year period ending in March 1953, the townspeople witnessed the coming and going of five different chiefs. One's tour of duty lasted a week before being handed his walking papers; another made it for almost two months—citing foot trouble as his reason for leaving. (Foot in the mouth?) And another—hanging in there for almost ten harrowing days failed to show up for work having been, "…called out of the city for an indefinite time."

The fourth and fifth chiefs' more credible reason for fleeing was that they didn't see eye to eye with the city manager over the police department's operation.

The *Sutherlin Sun* in an editorial entitled "Who's Next?" reported on the frequent changing-of- the-guard and pondered why.

In attempting to analyze the situation, the newspaper reported:

> …the outward appearance of the job of administering law enforcement in the city must be inviting to the applicants and none of the city chiefs have been without police experience, so only one other thing remains to be looked into as we see it, the administration of the position… the type of administration has everything but a healthy odor in our estimation.

The turnover of chiefs and the unhealthy odor's origin can be traced back to the end of the authoritarian reign of District Attorney Robert Davis.

Crusader Robert pulled the pin in April of 1952, and the first resignation by a Sutherlin police chief followed one month later. Handing in his badge was Chief Oliver Eggleston, who had held the chief's position for the previous two-and-a-half years. That in and of itself implies nothing sinister, unless you take into account that the next four chiefs sworn in then either resigned, came up missing, or were sent packing.

That tumultuous year represented the tug-of-war between the pro-gambling/prostitution factions and law enforcement. Davis proved relentless in his determination to enforce the law, and when he took office the good times that fed the county coffers were on their way out.

Remember that the tavern owners and others interested in keeping things the way they were B.D. looked to find qualified candidates to oppose Davis when he reran for office in 1951. Gerald Kabler, Sutherlin's attorney, who bid for the office was unsuccessful.

With Davis' departure, the city fathers had a vested interest in the return of gambling, and looked favorably upon Douglas County's vices as they bolstered the small towns' economies. And by lucky happenstance, somewhere along the line, the monetary rewards rippled out to the city politicians.

It would seem that rather than inept police chiefs, Sutherlin hired honest candidates intent on enforcing the law and unwilling to be pushed around.

By the end of that year, however, the situation received so much negative attention accompanied by too many embarrassing questions, that city management accepted the inevitable and gave up on arm twisting. Davis performed his job well, and it was tough for the vices to regain a toehold.

The churning of the chiefs ended when Richard Crumal took over the reigns of police chief in March 1953. Despite the tall order, Crumal held all the credentials and came well qualified to take on the delicate job of balancing law and order and dealing with city management. Whatever his pay, it couldn't have been enough.

Upon Audie Campbell's resignation in 1957, Crumal boasted to him that between the two of them they'd just about cleaned up the town.

Richard Crumal served as Sutherlin's police chief for eighteen years. During his tenure, he received numerous commendations from other law enforcement agencies, and enjoyed the respect and appreciation of the community.

CHAPTER TWELVE

The Best Seat in Town

From my privileged lookout on the second floor of Sutherlin's bank building, conveniently located on the corner of "where everything happened in town," I had an opportunistic view of much of the comings and goings of the general populace. This handy observation post just happened to be the law office of Gerald O. Kabler.

As described earlier, the bank building was adjacent to Jug's Club. Constructed in 1910, the structure was built using two different kinds of stones. The exposed sides facing south and east wore heavy rockcut stone quarried from an adjacent area, from which it was transported by rail to the building sight.

Like a prideful lady of minimal means who wears a beautiful silk dress on the outside, but conceals cheap cotton undies underneath, the west side and the back facing the alley were outfitted in brick and mortar

If, rather than making a left-hand turn at the corner and following Highway 99 northward, you instead journeyed straight on eastward one more block, you would have reached the end of the business area. Next, you passed the school's gymnasium/auditorium and merged into the country on the road known as Nonpareil Road.

The Office

Although less than plush, this law office, consisting of two small offices, was more than adequate. The front office, which served as the reception area, had three double-hung windows facing south. It was here that I greeted both happy and disgruntled clients.

From these south-facing windows, I could stand and gaze directly across the street at the dingy, flimsy curtains shading the second-floor rooms of the Sutherlin Hotel. On a warm day, with the windows open for fresh air, those thread-worn curtains unappealingly dangled out of the windows or flopped around in the summer breeze.

GERALD KABLER'S LAW OFFICES
The law offices with the author perched inside the window during a Fourth of July Parade, 1949.

Clients gained entry to Jerry Kabler's private office through a doorway centered in the common wall separating the two offices. Being the corner office, an expanse of windows faced south towards the hotel and eastward towards the end of town. In addition there was a stationary window set in the angled corner of the room. Who could ask for a better lookout tower than this?

Looking south onto Central Avenue from either the reception area or Mr. Kabler's office, I had the ability to observe everyone hustling along on the opposite side of the street and see who was driving through town—and with whom. I was afforded a view of anyone walking into the old hotel and, if arm-in-arm, with whom. Furthermore, I was able to pay attention to what patron was keeping her weekly hair appointment at Lucille's Beauty Nook, or who was getting his ears lowered in Riley Powers' barber shop. At a glance, I could note any shopper wandering in to pick up a prescription at Groshong's Drugstore, which was next door to the hotel.

With the early morning sun breaking through the east-facing windows, from my ringside seat I was able to scrutinize the horizon or casually watch customers purchasing gas or getting their air pressure checked in Nicolazzi's Service Station. Also, with a watchful eye, I could determine what trouble-maker was being hauled off to or released from the old jail across the street. It sat off to the north of the small alleyway beside Nicolazzi's Station.

And, less than a half block away, I had a bird's eye view of any patient hobbling or being helped into Dr. Grabow's office. And, if her condition was quite obvious, I'd guess how many more months Mrs. So-And-So had before delivery. Right across from Doc's office was Torrey's Hardware and Furniture. Maybe old-man Clemmons was walking away with a bag of nails and a gallon of paint.

Past the jail a few hundred feet and just north of Nicolazzi's Station was the U.S. Post Office. On most days, just about everyone in town found it necessary to wander in to pick up mail.

All in all, the odds were that on any given day, no matter what your errands in town, you'd be obliged to pass within sight of our windows.

Finding Our Nitch

Jerry Kabler had been practicing law about two years when I learned he was typing his own legal papers. Although I was 16 and still in high school, I hoped I could persuade him to hire me part time. If I could swing it, it would be my ticket out of the strawberry "killing fields."

Before I made my first visit to his office, I practiced and rehearsed my sales pitch designed to convince him he needed me—as a matter of fact, he'd be hardpressed to do without me!

Arriving at his office one Saturday morning, after introducing myself, I found him easy to approach, open, and friendly. I set about enlightening him as to my typing, shorthand, and bookkeeping skills. And if that wasn't good enough, I expounded on the "A" I'd received in Latin, which I assured him would be of value in helping me peel away the mystery of legalese.

Kabler's blue eyes sparkled with amusement as he patiently heard me out. At this point, he informed me that he really couldn't afford any help right then.

"I'm able to keep abreast of my own clerical work for the present but check back with me later."

As I nervously eased my way out the door, I made my final sales pitch. If he hired me for Saturdays and school holidays, he wouldn't be stuck in the office like he was that sunny Saturday. He'd be free to get out more often to play golf. Forget all my fantastic secretarial skills, I used the word "golf" as my secret weapon.

Getting my foot in the door, I made up my mind to show up on his doorstep often enough to at least convince him that, if nothing else, I had perseverance.

Before my second sashay into his office, the terrible thought occurred to me that he'd question his wife, Harriet Kabler, about my character, the status of my grades, and whatever else she might know. Not only had she been my English teacher, but at varying times she'd taught typing and shorthand.

Mrs. Kabler was a lovely, softspoken lady, and the daughter of one of Sutherlin's early settlers. Her gentle nature and inability to be a stern disciplinarian opened the door for her students to take advantage of her. But, she did have her limits and, on occasion, angrily sent me to cool my heels in the principal's office or study hall.

So, now I could worry about the chickens coming home to roost. Mrs. Kabler, I'm sure, knew about my recent expulsion from school, which came about because of the "three-strikes rule." Three unexcused absences and you were out. Mine were well-earned.

In order to reinstate a child into school, a parent had to show up at the principal's office to answer for their offspring's sorry sins. My poor mother, apprehensive, humiliated, and wondering where she'd gone wrong, made her appearance and the appropriate apologies.

I returned to school, missing only one day.

Now, and with good reason, I worried that I would be weighed in the balance and found wanting. After all, it was her husband I was badgering for a job.

Luckily, despite this tarnished past, I maintained good grades, as intermingled with my pursuit of fun, I did hit the books. Being a kind and generous soul, Harriet Kabler must have given her husband the nod because when I approached him again, he told me to come to work the next Saturday.

Little did I know, but I'm sure Mrs. Kabler did, that the same sporadic rowdiness and unladylike decorum that I sometimes exhibited would prove to serve me well. These same earthy traits should have been required attributes and prerequisites for working in that particular office at that particular time.

That spring, I began working in the law office all day Saturdays, school holidays, and after school as needed. By summer recess, Kabler's practice had picked up, and he asked me to work all summer. As I'd hoped, he'd grown accustomed to the luxury of leaving the office in my care so he could get out and play a few rounds.

Every so often on a Saturday, Mrs. Kabler dropped by the office. It was easy to see that she adored Jerry. Invariably, recalling some past misconduct, I'd suffer a brief twinge of guilt. Little did I know, however, that she grew genuinely fond of most of her students, and our sometimes unruly behavior and antics were a secret source of amusement to her.

Embarking on a law career and opening his first office at the age of 35, especially with two young children to support, was indicative of Jerry Kabler's grit and determination. He earned his law degree the hard way—struggling through the University of Oregon's law school while working for the Southern Pacific Railroad. By his own admission, it took ten years of juggling job, family, and school to complete his education.

Prior to making his life-altering decision to become an attorney, he taught and coached athletics at a few of the small schools that dotted Douglas County.

Jerry and Mrs. Kabler had two children, Carole Jo and Tommy (ten and four respectively), and Jerry delighted in calling them his little hellions. He loved children, and pridefully referred to his son, whose shenanigans earned him the nickname, "Terrible Tommy Kabler." It was not unusual to get a call at the office that Tommy had again

slipped away from home and was spotted at some off-limits site.

A huskily built man, he was gregarious and fun-loving. His salt-and-pepper hair was kept cut in the popular crewcut. Yet, this style failed to conceal the beginnings of a receding hairline and the inevitable thinning on top.

Mr. Kabler had a quick smile and a ready laugh. This hearty laugh was expelled and set into motion by tossing his head back when something tickled his funny bone. He was completely devoid of any pretentiousness; he was as down to earth as most of his clientele. These attributes endeared him not only to me but to his clients.

Getting it Together

My primary tool of the trade was a small, inefficient portable typewriter that Jerry salvaged from his college days. This lightweight typewriter was not meant for heavy use. Its keys were flat, metal-rimmed and stiff to the touch. It was anybody's guess as to where a given key might place its letter—high off the line or below the line. Being slow to respond to touch, it all too often imprinted strikeovers that made time-consuming corrections necessary, or the keys jammed. I spent as much time chasing the typewriter and pulling it back into place as I did typing. Each time I hit the carriage return lever, the portable followed the carriage, slowing working its way towards a left-hand plunge off the desk.

But, I couldn't argue with the fact that it served the purpose. We managed to pound out divorce complaints, logging contracts, complaints for monies, an occasional alienation of affection suit, income tax returns, and all called for documents and correspondence.

My dinky, second-hand desk sat in front of the door leading into Jerry's inner office. Just enough room remained between the back of my chair and his door for a client to pass behind me to gain entry.

Jerry's desk occupied the corner of his office where the common wall and the south wall met. An oak rolltop, it was crammed with a multitude of pigeonholes, nooks and crannies. The telephone took up a small spot near the windows.

Having acquired several glass-front bookcases, most of the space was already taken up with his meager, basic library of law books. One low-topped metal filing cabinet took care of his case files. This cabinet was hinged to open from the top, and inevitably I'd have to remove a partially smoked, soggy cigar before opening it.

Jerry loved a good cigar. Moving about the office, I'd find them half-smoked—their flattened ends chewed into a brown paste—teetering on the edge of a stack of files, balanced precariously on the edge of the filing cabinet, or perched on the top of the old rolltop.

You didn't need to observe him with a cigar to know he was a cigar-smoker. Telltale deposits of fine, gray ash were scattered around on the floor and sifted in amongst the papers piled on his desk.

To me, it seemed more effort than it was worth to go through the ritual of relighting those ugly used stogies. But, putting a match to the charred end, he'd draw on it and puff and puff waiting for that first sign of smoke. Sometimes it took several tries before he got it fired up.

Bursting the Bubble

As it so happened, it was here, atop the bank building, that my education was rounded out. Not only had my willing and enthusiastic instructor handed me the opportunity for a terrific hands-on business education; moreover, my mentor eagerly shared his more mature and advanced insight into human nature.

Furthermore, I became enlightened about the social workings of the town and got the inside scoop on those involved in the latest hanky-panky. I learned why so-and-so had filed for divorce, and who could-

n't or wouldn't pay his bills. Welcome to the real world.

The exploits other people whispered about or came by second or third hand, I acquired right from the horse's mouth. But it broke my heart since it did me little good as gossip material. I'd been cautioned early on that the number one rule of a law office is to keep your mouth shut!

Many a time I bit my tongue upon hearing the latest scuttlebutt making the rounds about a love-triangle and being unable to divulge what I knew to be the true titillating facts. Yet, with the passage of time, it became easier to keep my lip zipped.

Probably the biggest eye-popping shocker for me at that tender age came about when one of the town's businessmen instituted divorce proceedings against his wife. Now, it wasn't just that he initiated the filing, which in itself was unusual, but the wronged gentleman did have exceptionally well-founded grounds.

Although he tried to cushion the harsh facts by speaking soft and low, Mr. Kabler dropped a bombshell on me that exploded my limited view of the world. I don't think it did a lot for his either. You must keep in mind that we were right on the brink of and butting up to the nostalgic, everything's-perfect-in-suburbia-'50s.

I believe Jerry was caught offguard and unnerved by the husband's unsettling disclosure. So much so that he needed to share it with someone, so he confided in me, knowing it would be kept within those four walls.

It seems that the defendant wife—with whom the plaintiff had a small son—and the daughter of one of the local businessmen were involved in a lesbian relationship.

As soon as the words were out of his mouth, I could feel my face begin to turn red. I groped for a response, but nothing came. Making some nonsensical remark, I was too embarrassed to take the conversation any further.

I couldn't believe my ears. This just didn't fit neatly into the scheme of things. I'd heard about such affairs, however, not often. And besides, something like this happened in some weird, faraway place like Hollywood or San Francisco. That anything as foreign to us as this could go on in Sutherlin was beyond my wildest imagination.

I just knew I'd choke to death holding this breaking story. Not being able to tell a soul might even cause me to break out in blotchy, red hives. But keeping my own counsel held back the eruption. Down the road, I came to find it a reward in itself.

Recognizing both of these women by sight, they certainly didn't appear strange or different; actually they both seemed to be quite pleasant and "normal." Still, I couldn't shrug it off and wanted to bring the awkward subject back up with my boss and see where it led. But I was too embarrassed. Besides, having time to rethink it, I'm certain his sensitivity would have told him that this was offlimits for further discussion with me. Neither of us ever mentioned it again.

As it was, I learned another of life's lessons — not to take too much at face value, as all was not what it appeared to be!

Exposed to the real-life problems brought into the office, I witnessed first hand the damage and heartbreak inflicted on families by adultery, divorce, alcoholism, and lack of money to pay the bills.

For the first time, I watched tears well up in the eyes of a grown woman as she shakily signed her divorce complaint. For the moment, I felt helpless and ill-at-ease. Having no experience to draw from, I couldn't offer her a word of comfort or encouragement.

I knew the legal system would award her alimony and child support—empty decrees of the court as far as reality was concerned. If the husband wasn't especially tied to a bigbucks job, and found it inconven-

ient to pay (and most did), he'd just change jobs or skip town. Oh sure, she could haul him in for contempt—if she could find him—and seek another order requiring him to make up the back payments. But before she could initiate these proceedings, she had to find the money to pay her attorney up front. In most cases, it was throwing good money after bad.

A Woman's Place

For the most part, wives in the workplace in the forties and fifties were uncommon—at least after their contribution to the war effort. Those who did hold down a job were the exception to the rule, and after the first baby arrived, social convention decreed they quit. When the subject came up about a wife going to work, most men I knew laid down the law in no uncertain terms.

"Not my wife! She's not going to work!"

For many men of that era there was something demeaning about having a working wife. It implied that he couldn't support his family. For whatever reason, a woman who taught school seemed to be exempt from this disapproval. Probably because teaching wasn't considered a fulltime job.

Being the breadwinner, a man's worth was judged by how well he fulfilled this obligation. Furthermore, by reason of the fact that it fell to him to make the living, he benefited by having full say in most matters.

The majority of women didn't have any firm preparation for holding down outside jobs and were totally dependent on the kindness and generosity of their husbands. Should those qualities be lacking—well, you made your bed, so you slept in it.

The main rationale for sending a daughter away to college was not to see her graduate and land a high-paying job, but to land a college-educated husband. If a married woman worked, it was often taken for granted that it was for pin money, and she was paid accordingly.

By and large, women of that era and earlier times, had been sold a fairytale book of goods. It read that if you were a good girl and found your prince charming, then gave birth to two-plus children, you'd be fulfilled and live happily ever after. And, all the while your husband lovingly supported you and the children, was overtly happy, and remained forever faithful. This idealistic relationship was all well and good if both parties played by the same rules.

But, came the day when itchy feet got the best of him and he left for parts unknown, or he unexpectedly fell for another woman, the wife was left destitute. If he failed to comply with the terms of a divorce decree, or most times, even if he did, she was forced to find whatever menial work came her way to keep bread on the table. On the other hand, if it were an option, she could move back home and remain dependent.

Unhappily, I soon discovered that more often than not, that era's concept of married life was a myth shrouded in a mist of falsehoods—a fantasy castle built on quicksand.

For the Fun of It

Being an avid golfer, besides a doting father, Jerry made time every once in awhile to take Carole Jo along when he went to the Roseburg Country Club. Like a good Dad, he humored her by letting her try her hand at swinging a golf club. As it was, she showed promise and took to the game right away. Soon, he was shelling out money for golf lessons.

Several times, he returned from her lessons, followed by a short game, bursting with pride at how well she played. More than once, he told me, "The pro said Carole Jo's a natural!" As it so happened, my old boss had reason to be proud. Years down the road, both Carole Jo and Tommy became golf pros. After her marriage, Carole Jo's last name changed to Scala.

Golf wasn't Jerry's only recreation. As I mentioned, playing cards was high on his list of pastimes. Leaving the office without telling me his destination, or using the old standby, "I'm going to meet someone," implied to me where he might be found. I knew enough not to intrude upon this time unless it was an emergency, although the word "emergency" had never been defined. Therefore, I developed my own emergency criteria, one being a new prospective client who was getting tired of waiting and might decide to find an attorney in Roseburg.

It didn't happen too often, but determining that a matter was important enough to locate him, I'd hustle downstairs, round the corner of the bank and—cringing—pull open the door and peer into Jug's Club. Nothing and no one could have coaxed me beyond the doorway. I'd rather have taken my chances of walking on hot coals barefoot than tiptoeing into that dive.

As soon as you opened the door, you'd be hit by the deafening din that came from the wild and boisterous revelry inside. You couldn't have shouted loud enough from where I stood to be heard more than a few feet away. At the same time, the foul odor of stale beer assaulted your nose as though someone had slapped a beer-soaked washcloth over your face.

Not only did the place reek from the beer being downed that moment, but the stench mingled with years of spilt beer that had been absorbed into the pores of the beatup wood floor. For all intents and purposes, the flooring was well-preserved in alcohol.

You couldn't have asked for a better intercom system. Shouting to be heard, I'd inquire of the first man seated at the bar or standing near the door if he knew whether Mr. Kabler was in there. The pungent cloud of smoke hung like a blue fog, and made it next to impossible to see to the back of the room. Plus, as a rule, the joint was so packed with standing men that you couldn't see that far anyway.

This lack of visibility undoubtedly served to the advantage of anyone desirous of maintaining his anonymity. Not too many women, except maybe a raging, irate wife, had the guts to tromp to the back to see if her husband was holed up in there.

After my original inquiry, if the first gentleman didn't know the answer, he'd ask the guy a couple seats down. Someone towards the back would take up the call and yell, "Jerry in here?" Right away out of the foggy haze someone would relay, "Nope, not here."

Now, I really wouldn't have expected Kabler to fold a winning hand that instant, and maybe it wouldn't have been kosher right then to cash in his chips. Although I didn't have to hunt him down often, I'm sure one or two times he honestly wasn't there as reported. However, other times he miraculously showed up not long after the call went out over the intercom.

Running With the Big Dogs

On a couple of occasions, Mr. Kabler took up a stance by my desk with a mischievous look on his face. Out of the blue, and to my utter surprise, he encouraged me to punch him in the stomach as hard as I could. This was a new one on me. I'd had no prior coaching in pummeling before. Thinking he surely must be kidding, I shook my head. But he baited me on.

"Come on, hit me."

I reluctantly took a weak swing that didn't amount to much. I'd never punched anyone before and it went against the grain.

"Come on, do it again, but the next time harder!"

Next try, I put a little more into it, and, as he hoped, the blow bounced off causing my arm to spring back.

He grinned, obviously pleased with the result.

At first, I couldn't come to grips with what this routine was all about. But I came to realize he believed (and with good reason), that if you can't run with the big dogs, you'd better stay on the porch. For his own benefit, he needed to be sure that, should the occasion arise, he could hold his own. Those he associated with, whether in or out of the office, weren't bred or groomed to be lap dogs or fluffy poodles.

I don't know about outside of work, but Jerry's good conditioning paid off several times within the confines of the office. It wasn't unusual for a heated argument, bordering on becoming combative, to ensue downstairs in Jug's and end up in our office for resolution. Or maybe it was another partnership gone bad.

In any event, the office door would abruptly swing open, and in would tramp two or three disheveled testy loggers, gruffly inquiring, "Jerry in?"

The tension would be so heavy it rubbed off on me like carbon paper.

Shortly after admitting them into his office, I'd hear the men's harsh voices intermittently reaching a louder pitch, interjected with some rather choice and colorful profanities. Although Jerry was at his best as peacemaker, his mediating wasn't always successful. Sometimes, the arguing gained momentum or one of the unhappy gentlemen boldly took a swing or lunged at the other.

Knowing he could see it through, Jerry didn't hesitate to physically intervene by grabbing one of the men in an attempt to defuse the situation when common sense, tact, and diplomacy weren't cutting it.

Since my desk sat directly in front of his door stationed with my back to it, I was directly in the line of fire. I'd been caught off guard before with shoving and scuffling behind me as I tried to jump out of the way. Nevertheless, I'd become a quick study.

So when the yelling intensified, the language became more profane, and Jerry's voice began to rise in exasperation, I knew it was time to desert my post. My reaction time was flawless.

Pushed to the brink, and having a hold on one of the agitated scrappers, a steely-eyed Kabler, acting as his own bailiff, would wrench one of the men's arms into a half-nelson. As he jerked the door open, he shoved him through it. At the same time he grabbed another and physically escorted them to hell out of the office.

Unscathed and grinning, Jerry vigorously brushed his hands together signifying a job well done. I uttered some half-baked response. Pumped up from the unexpected workout and sideshow, we soon turned our attention back to whatever project occupied us before intermission.

The Stagger-Ins

Just because the appointment calendar showed few scheduled appointments, you couldn't take it for granted that you had a slow day on your hands.

Domestic squabbles originating in Jug's Club also stood a good chance of ending up in the law office. Maybe a woman, already fed up, found her old man in there drinking again. She'd had a belly full of the son-of-a-bitch coming home three sheets to the wind.

Or, perhaps a couple had been doing some serious drinking at the bar and a chance remark sparked an argument. As one of them jumped up, the squabble ended with the final words, "Fine, see if I give a shit, file for divorce! As a matter of fact, I'll escort you the hell up to Jerry's office—the sooner the better!"

Knowing it was only booze talking, Kabler would good-naturedly espouse a little down-to-earth counseling hoping to get them to kiss and make up. If it took hold, they'd soon sway out of the office arm-in-arm. Should his words of wisdom fall on deaf ears, one or the other would be back. The next time, there'd be a charge.

In any event, a small percentage of Jerry Kabler's business sprang from Jug's, much of it gratis.

Living Outside the Rainbow

The filing of Complaints for Monies against men employed in the mills or woods, and the concurrent garnishment of their wages, constituted a large part of our law practice.

Other than farming, there is probably not a more weather-dependent industry than logging. A logger must stand up to a double whammy. Not only are his earnings for the year dependent on the winter rainfall; to make matters worse, in the summer, he's at the mercy of the humidity—or lack thereof. The weather is an everyday question mark that affects his family's livelihood.

In Oregon, come early winter weather, it can rain off and on from September/October into May. Other years might not be that wet. Loggers always have their fingers crossed hoping for enough breaks in the drizzle so the logging roads will have a chance to dry out—at least enough so they can get back in the woods and yard out a few loads.

Since most of the roads are primitive and shaded by massive stands of trees, about the time they're passable, the rains hit again.

Then come summer, the humidity, being the amount of moisture in the air, stands as yet another stumbling block in the way of the money chase. This is because low humidity increases the fire danger.

Years back, all logging shows were obliged to have a humidity gauge at the landing. As the men went about their work, they kept a sharp eye on it. Because of the fire hazard, as soon as the humidity dropped to 30%, the law required that they shut down operations, load up their gear, and get out of the woods.

At 30% humidity, all it would take to start a fire in the dry underbrush could be the sparks from a chainsaw, from steel cables being drawn over rock, or from the exhaust of a loader or log truck.

John McWade, who retired in 1991 as District Forester for Eastern

Lane County and worked for the Oregon Department of Forestry for 42 years in forest fire prevention, explained:

> Humidity...affects the way open combustion occurs, the way forest fuels burn and the ease with which forest fires will start. The lower percent of moisture in the air, the better a fire will burn...At 30% humidity, fire danger is considered very high, and any number lower is considered extreme. Therefore, 30% humidity was the magic number that sent loggers home, and it has been since loggers have been able to read a thermometer.

This magic number specifically applied to Western Oregon. Eastern Oregon's logging regulations were somewhat different.

Two different methods were adopted by loggers in an attempt to circumvent the shortened work day brought about by low humidity. One was working what was appropriately called the "Hoot Owl Shift." (Yes, that was OWL.) This meant getting up at 3:00 or 3:30 a.m. and catching the crummy in the dark. If you were lucky, you could nod off on your boring ride to the job site. Your arrival at the landing was scheduled to meet the rising sun. From that minute on, the humidity gauge was the enemy.

Some days you might get in a full day's work, others might see you run out of the woods as early as 9:00 A.M. I recall days when upon reaching the woods, the men had to turn around and come back to town; the hostile humidity gauge already read 30% or less.

For the log trucker, for whom the bills always beckoned, it was also a rush against time. After getting his first load dumped at the mill and his trailer loaded, he made a mad dash back to the woods. Not to be deterred, the trucker was on a mission to get his second load before the men were run out of the woods. As it was for all logging equipment, the bank payments went right on whether the weather turned against you or not.

The second method of getting around the humidity gauge was to tinker with it—just a little. In order to gain a few more precious minutes to finish yarding in logs or loading a waiting truck, you could cover the gauge with a cold, wet cloth thereby raising the humidity reading. Then, should a forest ranger or fire warden appear on the scene, feigning absolute innocence and shaking your head, you could point to your gauge that showed you still had a little time yet.

Among other tricks used to keep the indicated humidity up, John McWade said he found several, including:

Hang the gauge by the creek

Hose down the adjacent area

Slide the scale on a cheap thermometer

Hang the gauge in a powder box and cover it with a wet sock

In theory, loggers worked hard all summer and struggled to put money away for the inevitable winter downtime. His rainy-day savings were supposed to see him through the winter until the spring start-up of logging. For most, however, the reality was starkly different. It took all summer to catch up on the bills that piled up over the previous winter.

Then, about the time he got those bills paid, another winter stared him in the face. It began all over again—running up tabs until the next spring. It was a continual game of trying to play catch up, and it was a game the majority of small gypo operators and their employees could never quite win.

Unlike loggers, the mill workers stood a better chance of year-round employment. Although, the gypo mill operator and his employees were, to a certain extent, more prone to winter cutbacks.

The majority of large mills had stockpiled in their cold-decks a sufficient inventory of logs for processing during the winter. The more board feet of logs in the cold-deck, the better the outlook for winter-long pay checks.

Those timber workers unable to get even or catch up on their bills, were the reason delinquent accounts got turned over to Kabler for collection.

Generally, the debtholder willingly let an outstanding account run through the winter. But come summer, his patience ran out if the debtor chose to ignore him or failed to make payment arrangements.

As a rule, I felt sorry for the poor fellow whose wages were garnisheed. Still, facing harsh reality, small businesses were unable to carry a large amount of debt on the books. Moreover, with work available most anywhere in the state, it was too easy for the footloose and fancy free to pick up and move, leaving the businessman holding the bag.

The Race Against Time

The eerie wail of an ambulance racing in from the east served to interrupt business as usual and summoned us to the east-facing windows. Since Weyerhaeuser kept its ambulance garaged at the camp, we just about knew for sure that it would be its ambulance transporting one of its employees.

Or, maybe the Roseburg ambulance had been called and dispatched to an accident on another logging show. If that were the case, the ambulance had already caught the eye of people along main street when it ate up the road through town. Timing its return back to town, an alert observer might make a calculated guess as to the accident site.

No matter the circumstances, this shrill siren turned heads, bringing everyone to attention. Was the injured man a friend or family member? Should it be the Weyerhaeuser ambulance, we waited at the window to see if it squealed to a stop in front of Dr. Grabow's office. Maybe, early on someone thought Doc could handle the emergency. Or at least, better stabilize the man until they reached the emergency room.

All it might take would be an educated glance for Doc Grabow to wave the driver on to the hospital. If this were the case, the ambulance would barely slow at the stop sign, then rush southward twelve miles to the Roseburg Hospital.

The ambulance's destination depended on the level of surgical resources available at either Roseburg's or Eugene's hospital. If the blood-stained logger had suffered a mutilated limb or other obvious life-threatening trauma, or his body was otherwise mangled and shattered, the emergency vehicle would make a turn northward to Eugene. Sitting on pins and needles for the next 60 nail-biting miles, the driver clenched his steering wheel as he did his best to make good time over windy two-lane Highway 99. He took every curve as fast as he dared and floored it on every straightaway. His patient's chances looked pretty slim; he could succumb to shock or hemorrhage to death before they reached the hospital door.

In certain cases, Eugene's hospital possessed essential medical equipment that was unavailable in Roseburg and could provide a higher level of care for trauma patients. And most importantly, it retained on staff the vital qualified surgeon needed. Sometimes a patient transported to Roseburg was treated, stabilized, and later transferred to Eugene by ambulance.

With any major injury every minute counts. Being injured in the woods meant having two strikes against you for starters.

"You're not out of the woods yet," was not an idle expression where we lived.

After graduation, I settled in working for Jerry Kabler full time. I loved the work, and couldn't imagine doing anything more interesting. Besides divorces, wills, logging contracts, and the miscellaneous matters that comprise law office business, we filled in by doing income taxes during tax season, and kept books for a few businesses, including the Pastime tavern and restaurant. I still found plenty of time to get up from my desk for a break and idly gaze out the window. During the spring and summer, this was partly a matter

WIDOW-MAKERS & RHODODENDRONS

of trying to stay awake. Those windows provided our only source of air conditioning and ventilation.

Being only one business away from the entrance to Jug's, my open upstairs windows allowed the sounds from the tavern to bleed into the office. This held especially true on Saturdays. With every opening and closing of the tavern door the plaintive refrains from Eddie Arnold's or Ernest Tubb's song about a love gone bad, or Jimmy Wakely and Margaret Whiting bemoaning their fear of being found while "Slippin' Around," would drift upstairs within my hearing. Rather than distracting, I found it a pleasant diversion from the roar of the truck traffic.

From my crow's nest, day after day I could watch one after another loaded log trucks roar in from the east. Making the dirt and asphalt roads they traversed tremble, they were en route to whatever mill in the area had contracted to purchase the logs.

This routine hum of traffic, the muffled noise sporadically emitting from the merriment from Jug's, and the noisy roar of the log trucks all blended together to form a background of sound as Jerry Kabler and I endeavored to oil the wheels of justice and insure the integrity of the judicial system within our town.

— 138 —

— P A R T F O U R —

✶ ✶ ✶

END OF THE LINE

CHAPTER THIRTEEN

Out of the Timber, Not Out of the Woods

And so they paraded in from the east, load after load of Douglas fir piled high on the trucks and trailers. Pieces of loose bark, chunks of dirt, and gritty fine dust flew off the immense logs and littered the street as they made their way through town. Rumbling along were GMCs, Whites, Diamond Ts, Cornbinders (Internationals), and an occasional ratty-looking converted used army truck, all loaded to the limit and more. Many of the rigs were owned by independent truckers, whose names were proudly handlettered on the doors.

With a comforting rhythm, each driver skillfully downshifted, slowing his mammoth rig to a minimum crawl in preparation for the stop sign by Nicolazzi's Service Station. After coming to a full stop, the majority of drivers eased their truck straight on through the intersection. As they moved right along, the pleasant aroma of freshly cut fir and cedar permeated the air.

Rolling on down Central, as the drivers dexterously shifted through their gears, you could about bet they'd spot a familiar face on the street to honk at or wave to. At the end of the block, the trucks either continued straight ahead to one of the mills near the railroad tracks or made a left turn and traveled south to one of the many mills on Highway 99.

A few of the trucks, upon reaching the stop sign by Nicolazzi's made a right turn and traveled on northward three more miles to Martin Brothers Box. Situated in the neighboring town of Oakland, Martin Box was one of the larger employers in the area. The company manufactured wire-bound shipping containers.

Coming in from the opposite end of town, trucks bearing their weighty payload approached the stop sign before merging onto Highway 99. Here again their destination depended on the species of logs being hauled. A few went on to Martin Brothers Box. But, the majority made a right turn on Highway 99, and like those entering from the east, headed south to one of the beckoning sawmills.

The Rat Race

That one block of Highway 99 running through Sutherlin was the busiest block in town for shopping or guzzling. But during the summer, all manner of truck traffic dominated the scene. Besides the loaded trucks, the empty rigs returning from the mills roared back through town bound for the woods. With their log trailers piggybacked and chained down to the trucks' bunks, the drivers rushed like bats out of hell to get back to the landing in hopes of a second load for the day. If they hustled, they might squeeze in a third. In the heat of the summer, they knew they were pressing their luck. This held especially true if the reading on the landing's humidity gauge had begun to drop before the driver left with his first load.

A notice running in the *Sutherlin Sun* in the summer of 1945 would seem to have sprung from this scrambling. The notice, with "County Court" typewritten at the bottom, offered a $50.00 reward, "For information leading to the conviction of any driver of a logging truck driving recklessly or at an excessive speed over County Oiled Road running east of Sutherlin."

Like the entire timber industry, the loggers, truckers, and sawmill workers in the Sutherlin area worked at full steam in their effort to fill the insatiable demand for lumber. Each day, hundreds of thousands of board feet of logs moved through the center of this town to the awaiting mills. Day and night sawdust belched and spewed from the mills' burners, some days clinging to and spoiling the housewives' freshly hung wash.

The Pond and Beyond

Now into the homestretch, each truck and its cargo arrived at the contracting mill and pulled up to the small scale shack. Here the scaler scaled the logs to determine the number of board feet in the load. At the same time, he graded the logs to set their value.

While the scaler made his determinations, the trucker removed either one or two center binders (whichever was required at the time) that secured his load. The remaining two would be removed just before dumping.

Most large sawmills had an adjacent pond into which the logs were dumped. At first glance, some of these mill ponds looked like a small lake. Sutherlin Timber Products, located just south of town and another major employer, boasted a mill pond covering 20 acres.

After the trucker received his scale sheet, he pulled the truck ahead to the brow log fastened at the edge of the pond. The brow log is a huge anchored, sturdy, squared-off log, the top of which is level with the truck's bunks. A brow log could also take the form of a large cement block poured specifically for that purpose. In either case, strong, heavy steel cables were permanently fastened to it.

The free ends of the cables attached to the brow log were tightly bound under and around the load. The trucker loosened the binders and knocked out the cheese blocks on the pond side of the trailer. Cheese blocks were wedgeshaped blocks used to hold the big logs of that day on the trailer. The load was winched off and, with a thunderous splash, dumped in the pond.

The agile pond man, wearing caulk boots to grip the thick bark, balanced himself atop the floating logs. Using a long pole called a pike pole, he guided them over to the opposite side of the pond. There, a crane operator lifted them out of the water and piled them onto the cold-deck—much the same as you would heap wood onto a wood

SAWMILL AT WORK, 1940s
Pond monkeys using pike poles to move logs up chute into mill. A
strong stream of water removes debris as they are pulled upward.
Concrete brow log shown in foreground.

pile. It should be noted that at the larger mills, the pond man's job could include cutting the floating logs to length using a drag saw.

✳   ✳   ✳

Unless you work in the office, absolutely no job having anything to do with logging or logs is anywhere near safe. The pond man's job is no exception.

Hopping from one log to another to get around the pond, he could take a tumble. Even if he could swim, the logs he took a dive between might close over him. Also, the chance existed that he could hit his head on another log when he fell and be knocked unconscious and drown.

Or if the man wasn't a swimmer and tried to pull himself up onto a floating log, the log would just spin and roll with each attempt. The answer to this was to work his way down the log to the buttend. Once there, he could pull himself up onto it. And don't forget his weighty caulk boots!

Yet, sometimes it's the unexpected that takes you out.

April 21, 1950 *Sutherlin Sun*

> Warren Freeman, 62, a resident of Sutherlin...was killed Monday afternoon while working at the mill pond at the Rock Island Lumber Co...Freeman was working on a pile of logs which suddenly shifted. He was thrown 25 feet into the water, where he struck a floating log....Death was reported to have been caused by concussion rather than drowning.

Even today, the cold-decks are fascinating to behold. Imagine the largest wood pile you've ever seen. Magnify this hundreds and hundreds of time. Rather than a small log from the woodpile measuring six to ten inches in diameter, you have a pile of logs each measuring four feet in diameter—some much more. These giants are stacked one on top of another, and reach upwards to a height of 75 feet, with 60 to 65 feet being considered the most efficient. The

CRANE STACKING LOGS ON COLD-DECK
Photograph circa 1950.
Photograph courtesy of the Douglas County
Museum of History and Natural History.

reason for this is that in extracting the logs from the cold-deck less breakage is apt to occur when kept to that height.

Saving for a rainy day, a large mill might have ten rows of these giant woodpiles held in reserve for winter milling. During the hot summer months, an overhead sprinkler system keeps a spray of water raining down on the cold-decks. This prevents the logs from cracking and splitting.

If the logs were not to be cold-decked, the pond man guided and pushed the logs with his pike pole towards the mill. A chain-driven chute called a log haul propelled the log into the mill and through the cutoff saw where the ends are squared and cut to length. If this process had already been completed in the pond, its first destination would be the head rig saw.

From that point, the log moved along on the transfers and conveyers for processing through the multipurpose saws, and sometimes a resaw, until the product produced by that mill was out the door. Whether plywood, studs, lumber, or other useful wood products, the job was completed when stacked in the yard ready for shipment.

Murphy's Law might be challenged, but it was always upheld and in full force and effect in the sawmill environment. Despite Oregon and Washington's joint passage of stringent regulations regarding mill safety in the early 1920s, the mills within the time-frame of the 1940s and early 1950s remained fraught with danger. In many cases the technology was not available to fully implement many of the required safety features.

The mills continued to hide any number of ways to mangled or maimed.

HEADRIG, 1940s
Squaring off a log in the Roseburg mill.
Photograph courtesy of Roseburg Forest Products

A sampling of the hazardous work conditions that existed were:

❋ No protective covers over the fast-spinning saws. This left you vulnerable to have body parts terrifyingly intermingled with the highspeed, razorsharp saws. This held particularly true for the small mill operations. At larger mills, an ingenious employee might improvise guards or hoods.

Sawmill accident reported in September 15, 1950 *Sutherlin Sun:*

Wilfred L. Vian 33, a partner in the Vian Bros. sawmill located southwest of the Sutherlin airport, was instantly killed Wednesday afternoon when he fell into the saw. . . . The saw struck Vian in the head and left shoulder.

It was reported that Vian was working alone at the time of the accident, and his nephew found him shortly thereafter. With no one there to shut down the saw, one can only imagine the horror that greeted the nephew upon his arrival back at the mill. Few sawmill deaths were neat and tidy.

GRADING AND SORTING, 1940s
Photograph courtesy of Roseburg Forest Products.

❋ No protective covers over the rapidly rotating belts and pulleys that ran the whirling saws; before you knew it, loose clothing could get caught up in these. In the blink of an eye, a finger, hand, or for that matter an arm could be agonizingly mangled or completely severed if drawn into a pulley or roller before the machinery could be shut down.

But, being mindful of these dangers, and chilled by other's horror stories, the mill workers used common sense and took preventive measures to protect themselves as best they could.

They knew better than to work around operating machinery with their shirttail hanging out, or their sleeves unbuttoned and left to dangle at their wrists. Caution dictated that clothing fit snugly against their body. Using safety pins, a mill worker pinned and caught up the fullness in his sleeves, thereby tightly binding them around his arms. Others improvised by slipping metal bicycle clips around their arms. This worked for bike riders who clamped them around the bottom of their pant legs to keep them out of the bicycle chain. And it worked for the mill workers, too.

❋ While moving along on the conveyer through the various saws, a large knot in a log might cause it to hang up on a saw tooth, or some other mishap could cause a giant slab, plank or timber to be flipped off the carriage and propelled into your work area. This would happen so fast, there was little chance of jumping out of the way. More than likely the best you'd end up with would be a broken or shattered leg, a smashed foot, or both.

❋ Many of the sawyers were compensated by the number of board feet they processed for the week. This monetary incentive often parlayed into hasty processing. Each worker along the line was pushed to the limit in his attempt to keep up.

It could be argued that this ram-rodding was the catalyst for all sorts of accidents.

The wearing of goggles to protect the eyes was not mandatory. Nevertheless, some workers' jobs exposed them to whirling clouds of sawdust most of the day. Out of self-defense, these fellows might slip on a pair of goggles to prevent the constant irritation to their eyes.

While still in high school, the grim reality of what could happen to unprotected eyes within the mill hit close to home. Murray Welch, the father of one of my friends and classmates, lost an eye working in one of Sutherlin's mills. He was working on the main saw cutting through a log when, quicker than the blink of an eye, a sharp snag flew off. This errant projectile, struck him directly in the eye, and like a knife piercing an olive, put out his eye.

Ironically, years later he lost the other eye in a bar room fight. Up until a short time prior to Murray's death in 1981, he ran the concession stand in the Douglas County Courthouse in Roseburg. His seeing eye dog, Asa, was always by his side.

No rules were in place mandating the wearing of ear plugs to prevent damage to mill workers' ears. These workers on every shift were exposed to the constant screaming saws and incessant deafening roar of the mill. Some workers who couldn't stand this earsplitting racket stuffed cotton in their ears. That helped some, but not enough.

Many retired sawmill workers can trace their hearing loss back to this unrelenting exposure.

Offloading With a Twist

For the log truck driver, dumping the logs at the mill pond completed the job that began in the woods. Nevertheless, an occasional small mill lacked a contiguous pond. This necessitated the use of a fork lift to either lift the logs up and off the truck or shove the load off onto the ground.

The truckers disliked this manner of offloading, and with good reason. In the course of transporting the logs over rough terrain, the load could have shifted somewhat, making the logs less stable than when loaded.

When the trucker offloaded at the mill pond, heavy steel cables were first bound around the load before the trucker removed the remaining chains and binders. But in depositing the logs on the ground, he pushed his luck. In order to remove the wraps, he was obliged to stand directly under the tons of logs, one of which might be offkilter or unbalanced.

As he released the wraps, he anxiously monitored the load keeping a wary eye out for any ominous sign of instability. If a log showed the slightest sign of movement, he had to be prepared to drop the wraps, turn, and run like hell, or take a dive under the trailer.

Tragically, all too often someone was caught off guard when he averted his eyes for a single moment. The sentence for not being quick on your feet was most likely death. Being smashed and pinned under the weight of a huge log does away with a variety of alterative results.

It could so happen that when the log crashed, he was almost out of the way; maybe it only trapped his legs beneath its weight. He could live for the day when he might walk again. But these were not the days of medical miracles.

As a footnote and by way of hammering home the sad and disgraceful manner in which the deaths of timber workers were treated, I offer the following facts:

The Vian fatality reported September 15, 1950, was judged undeserving of a bold, large type, attention-getting headline. It did get a place at the top of the front page, squeezed in between the two real headliners of the week.

To the left of the Vian report, the big bellringer spelled out in large bold type told how the Sutherlin High School Bulldogs trounced

Roseburg's number two team and Myrtle Creek, thereby placing the Bulldogs in the finals.

To the right of the trifling fatality, also in large, bold, eyecatching type, was the sky-is-falling notice that the vote on water bonds was to take place that day—so get out and vote.

Making this even more shameful—yes, that is possible—directly beneath the reported Vian death, was the news of another fatality for the week. The caption for this no-great-shakes accident was also in small, nondescript print. This time it was a 38-year-old logger killed by a falling limb while employed as a bucker. Another ho-hum event.

These two fatalities weren't isolated incidents that took place at work sites at different outposts around the state of Oregon. These men were not itinerant nobodies. Both were young family men. Vian left a widow and family in Yoncalla, a town just north of Sutherlin. The logger had called Sutherlin home for eight years. He left a widow and four children.

Two gory and brutal on-the-job fatal accidents in one week in a burg the size of Sutherlin. Where was the outrage? A person would think that, at the very least, the hometown newspaper would find it appalling enough to warrant an attention-getting headline. One that screamed to the high heavens about the carnage taking place right under the good townsfolk's noses.

But instead, as in most logging accidents, these deaths were treated in an offhand and callous manner. Why make much ado about nothing?

CHAPTER FOURTEEN

Hats Off

No book is complete without the reader learning what became of the folks central to the story. So let's begin with the ragtag bunch of kids that fate threw together in this less than charming little town.

Whatever Happened to?

In the class of 1949, our Freshman year began with 39 students. We graduated with a class of 26. Of the missing 13, some moved away, some fell by the wayside, and a few joined the armed services.

The girls, unaware that women's lib was down the road a ways, took up the traditional role of homemaker and set about having babies. Those who held jobs worked their way up the ladder to better-paying ones, some in banks or government jobs, while at the same time raising families.

Those schoolmates who joined the service were either caught in the Korean War or joined because of the War. Four, including Kenneth Briscoe from my class, failed to return home.

Those high school sweethearts who married right out of school, or within a year or two, beat the odds in a surprising number. A greater-than-could-be-expected number have celebrated their 50th wedding anniversaries, and others are only a few years short of it. The reason quite a few didn't hang together for that milestone is because death intervened.

The boys did well. In our class, we ended up with two CPAs, an aeronautical engineer, and a college instructor. Others began businesses of their own, remained working in the timber industry, or found other jobs more to their liking. The real brain of our class, Chris Bachman, apparently never looked back and no one knew what became of him. From the only lead I ran down, it seems he was involved in some form of research at M.I.T. and died in midlife.

From the graduating class the year ahead of ours, one graduate became a mortician, expanding his business into the Musgrove Family Mortuary in Eugene, and another a geologist. One fellow became an attorney and later retired as a Municipal Court Judge. Others latched onto jobs, working their way up to managerships. One girl became a nurse.

No one ended up in jail.

And whatever happened to those Firman boys that cruel fate dropped in Sutherlin? After graduation, Dick tried millwork and discovered there had to be a better way. He enrolled in college, became a teacher, and taught at a state college in Washington.

At one of our few school reunions, Dick jumped all over himself to boast about his brother's accomplishments. Impressed with what he told me, I later contacted Don Firman via Dick.

I believe Don represents the best in all of us. He didn't decry life's adversities. He knew what he wanted and set about doing whatever it took to accomplish it.

I hope you feel as privileged to read his letter as I do in sharing it with you.

Jeddah, Saudi Arabia
Saturday, 23 March 1991

I must apologize for the long delay in writing. Dick gave me your letter over six months ago, and asked me to write to you. I've been fairly busy since...Now that the war is over [The Gulf War], I've a little more leisure time...

I think about Sutherlin quite often....When I look back I realize how lucky I am, how lucky we all are, to have experienced the freedom of a semi-frontier environment during our most precious years. I especially remember my high school years and how much of my life was shaped by people and events in such a short time during that magical transition from child to adult. I'm convinced that during the trying periods of ones life, those fond memories give us strength.

Let me give you a short resume of my life after high school. After graduation....I worked in some of the local sawmills to save money for flying lessons and college. As far back as I can remember, I've always wanted to be an Air Force officer and pilot. The influence of World War II probably had a lot to do with that desire. At that time the Korean War was on and the United States Air Force required two years of college to enroll in their Aviation Cadet Program, leading to USAF Pilot Wings and a commission as 2nd Lieutenant.

In the Fall of 1952, I enrolled at Santa Rosa Junior College in Santa Rosa, California, to complete the two year college requirement. After one and a half years, the USAF lowered the prerequisites for the Aviation Cadet program to a high school diploma and I immediately applied. I passed all of the entrance exams with flying colors and in March 1954 was off to Lackland Air Force Base, San Antonio, Texas for Preflight Training.

Fifteen months later, I graduated from USAF Pilot Training at Laredo AFB, Texas. And, I must say, that June day in 1955, when I received my Gold Bars and Silver Wings, was the most thrilling event of my life.

The next 20 years of my life were spent in one of the most exciting and rewarding careers a man could hope for. There were numerous assignments throughout the United States with short periods of temporary duty overseas. However, the greatest thing that ever happened to me was my assignment to Plattsburgh AFB, New York, where I met my future wife, Karen...After a six-month engagement, we were married....It takes a special woman to marry an Air Force pilot and raise their three children almost singlehanded. . . I shall always be grateful for her love and devotion to the family.

I served my entire career in the Strategic Air Command flying tankers, except for a combat tour in Vietnam as an RF101 Voodoo pilot, flying reconnaissance missions. My last assignment was in Sault Ste Marie, Michigan, where I retired in 1974 as a Lt. Colonel.

Because of my air refueling experience, I was hired by the Boeing Company to instruct Imperial Iranian Air Force pilots in the operation of the 707 tanker. In June 1974 I moved the entire family to Tehran, Iran and enjoyed three wonderful years in the exotic Middle East. In June, 1977, it was back to the Pacific Northwest, but this time near Seattle…

I've always loved small airplanes, so decided to try that for awhile. I worked as Assistant Chief Pilot and Chief Pilot for a local Fixed Base Operator. It was fun but not much pay and the hours were atrocious. In February 1979, I decided to go back to heavy jets and took a position as Captain on a B707 with a Seattle Charter Company. That was a real challenge and the pay was adequate. I thoroughly enjoyed it, but this was the Recession of '79 and the company went bankrupt. Flying jobs were almost impossible to find.

However, in the summer of 1980, I discovered that Saudi Arabian Airlines was looking for B707 captains, to be based in Jeddah, Saudi Arabia. I was accepted for that position and in September 1980, I started my career with Saudi Arabian Airlines. Adjustment to an extremely different culture was not easy. But I survived and had the privilege to upgrade to the Lockheed L1011 TriStar and the Boeing 747.

I've been flying in command of a B747 for the past five years and consider it the safest and most reliable aircraft I've ever flown. My plan is to retire from flying in October 1992 and go back to [Washington].

Once you've scaled the wall of doubt, all other obstacles are minute.

A Follow up on Persons, Places & Things:

—Affectionately known in the community as Mr. Golf, in 1964, Gerald Kabler became Oregon District Court Judge for Douglas County. Upon his death in 1980, the *NewsReview* reported: "His courtroom was known to be efficient if somewhat unorthodox for his personable and humorous approach."

—Dr. and Mrs. Grabow are deceased.

—Robert Davis, the zealous District Attorney, was blessed with the talent and drive that lead people to great accomplishments. He'd made a name for himself locally, which is how state and federal politicians begin their careers. After leaving the District Attorney's office he came into the law firm of Orcutt, Long & Neuner where the author worked.

With Mr. Orcutt's retirement, the firm became Long, Neuner & Davis. Not long after that, he was sworn in as a Circuit Court Judge of Douglas County. He thereafter wound up in Salem as Executive Assistant to Governor Tom McCall. He made it to Washington, D.C. for a short time.

He and his wife, Jeanne, divorced. According to his exwife from there he took several executive business positions, remarried three or four times, got into financial trouble, and in the end "never made much of himself" at least considering the direction in which he had taken off. He is now deceased.

—One year short of the new millennium in which he hopes to celebrate his centenarian birthday, Walter "Turk" Manning, Oakland's historic police chief, proved he was still a force to be dealt with. In the process of remodeling Oakland's City Hall, the bell that Turk installed back in the mid-1950s to signal the ten o'clock curfew, was removed. The Oakland Historical Museum requested that the city donate the bell to the museum. Upon getting wind of this, Turk let out a resounding peal claiming he had bought and paid for the bell and it was his since the city had neglected to reimbuirse him. Following a brief investigation, the City Council unanimously concluded that Turk's claim was true.

The bell will be installed in Manning's backyard "where it belongs." Maybelle Manning, Turk's 90-year-old wife speaking on his behalf, exclaimed, "Walt said they never gave a damn about it before, so why do they now? Walt doesn't pull his punches, he says what he thinks."

—Kenneth Ford was an American success story. But unlike some millionaires, he didn't make it on the backs of his employees. Mr. Ford, a shy man who shunned publicity and loathed pretension, worked longer and harder than his employees. He was appreciative of those who put in a honest day's work for an honest dollar.

Roseburg Forest Products, which began as Roseburg Lumber Company, went on to become the largest privately held company in Oregon, and one of the largest in the United States. At one time 5,000 people worked at Ford's operations in Oregon and California.

As far back at 1957, Kenneth Ford set up a charitable foundation to help those in need. But even earlier and as far back as 1951, he was contributing sizable amounts to the community. Later The Ford Family Foundation, a multimillion dollar charity, was launched and became one of the 50 largest philanthropic funds in the nation. Many of the gifts from the foundation are given anonymously.

—On May 26, 1995, the author attended a ceremony in Brookings, Oregon, where the Japanese pilot, Nubuo Fugita, returned for the fourth time to the site of his bombings. At a ceremony held in the public library he placed his family's samurai sword on display. Interpreted by a relative, his words to the those in attendance were:

"When I came here to bomb, I thought I would die in this place, but fortunately I lived and was able to return to Japan. When I came here [the first time after the War] I found that the people were so nice, I thought that even if I had died, somebody would have collected my bones and returned them to Japan. Instead I was able to return and see what a wonderful community this is. I always wanted to be friendly with the people here all of my life."

Fugita died in 1997 at the age of 85. A close friend in Brookings said of him, "He was so very sorry. He had very, very deep regrets."

Fugita always considered Brookings to be his spiritual home. When he returned in 1992 to mark the 50th anniversary of the attack, he planted a redwood tree at the bombsite.

A year after his death, according to his wishes, some of his ashes were deposited near the attack site.

—In the mid-1990s, six cherry trees were planted at the simple stone monument erected in 1950 outside of Bly, Oregon. This monument was dedicated to the six victims killed by the Japanese balloon bomb that exploded in May of 1945.

You will recall that Japanese schoolgirls made up a large percentage of the work force involved in assembling the paper incendiary balloons. Japanese children from the Fukuga Elementary School donated the trees.

—The official closing of Weyerhaeuser's Camp Sutherlin logging operations occurred in January of 1961. The original camp was razed and the railroad tracks torn out. All logged timberland was reforested through Weyerhaeuser's tree farm program.

—On January 16, 1961, twelve years to the day after transporting the first load of logs from Camp Sutherlin, Old Steam Engine #100 was retired. Sometime later, with donations from Sutherlin's civic organizations, she was restored. The shiny black engine and her red caboose now hold a place of honor in Sutherlin's park.

—The old Sutherlin Hotel was torn down, and a modern bank building sits in her place.

—The generation of Parazoos that included Doug, Brad and Shannon have all passed on, with the exception of one remaining sister. If we ever again have a need for that breed of tough, individualistic, and independent men, I wonder who's gong to fill their shoes.

—Jug's club is gone. A gift and floral shop occupies the premises. If other-worldly entities do exist, ghosts of patrons past must wander about this shop confused and dazed—one inquiring of another, "Are you sure we're in the right place?"

And What About the Timber Industry?

Because of acknowledged past environmental damage brought about by logging, new technological innovations have been and continue to be implemented so as to prevent damage to the forests' ecosystem.

Stringent OSHA safety regulations have been put into place to benefit loggers and mill workers. These are in addition to those mandated by the state of Oregon and the timber industry itself.

Still, according to the Occupational Safety & Health Division of the U. S. Department of Labor, logging remains the nation's most dangerous occupation. For a five-year average ending in 1996, the fatality rate for the timber industry was four times higher than in the mining sector.

The use of helicopters for yarding logs out of the woods is being employed by a few larger logging companies. But, at the cost of 3.5 million dollars per copter, where does that leave the little guy? Does he go the way of the mom and pop corner store? Or perhaps he would be the ideal candidate for the other suggested alternative method of logging—the return to yesteryear's mule and horse logging.

Horse logging is being used on some private lands not for what the horses do, but what they don't do. They don't tear up the ground, and they definitely don't give off sparks or start fires. They also have greater maneuverability through thick timber than do machines.

Oregon law requires reforestation following timber harvesting. Replanting or seeding must begin within 12 months after harvesting and be completed within 24 months.

Ongoing research continues looking towards producing "super trees." These would be genetically engineered to grow faster and be more disease resistant.

OLD ENGINE #100
Located in Sutherlin's City Park.
Photograph courtesy of Bert Webber, Webb Research Publishers.

As for the sawmills, gone are the wigwam waste burners adjacent to each roaring mill. What used to go into the burner now becomes decorative bark, sawdust, and chips. Whatever part of a log is not used for lumber is processed into another useful product. Nothing is wasted.

Sawmills have been modernized. Computer-driven systems use laser technology to scan the logs to determine where to cut so as to obtain the most lumber out of each.

Mills have geared up with equipment that accommodates logs no larger than 24 inches, where before logs measuring 108 inches were the norm. State of the art technology has resulted in smaller work forces.

Privately, many logging companies and mills own and manage their own forests.

Change hangs in the air in just about every aspect of dealing with our forests.

Few young people in logging country any longer look to the timber industry as a place to spend their working lives. And the continual layoffs of workers reinforce that decision.

The new generation of loggers, or forest managers, have become better educated and more environmentally sensitive. For one, Oregon State University offers logger education extension programs that cover forest ecology, natural resource issues and silviculture. This program is designed for the education of loggers as the applied ecologists of the future.

Community colleges in timber country offer programs whereby loggers are learning new skills to keep them in the woods, working more as caretakers of the forest.

Displaced loggers and mill workers are also entering retraining programs looking towards work outside of the timber industry.

And let's not forget, loggers themselves are avid outdoorsmen who love to hunt and fish. With new awareness, they work to minimize

OUR LADY LOGGER, JODI OTTEN
Seen here with her Belgian draft horses weighing between 1,800–2,250 pounds each. In 1976, divorced with 5 children, this gutsy lady combined her love of horses with a way to make a living. Jodi's "For Hire" ad read: "Little or no soil compaction, erosion, or damage to residual trees." She consistently placed first or second in Draft Horse Weight Pulling contests throughout Oregon.

damage to the land. They want the wildlife, fishing streams, creeks and rivers to remain clean and pristine for their enjoyment as well as future generations.

A Perspective of Another Time and Place

Keep in mind, that at the time during which loggers have been accused of raping the forests and destroying the land, the word "environment" was not on everyone's lips, nor did it generate the immediate controversy it does today. No one could have foreseen the time when the "inexhaustible forests" of the Pacific Northwest might be endangered.

The "E" word may have appeared in a biology textbook. Other than that, it would have been about as foreign to that generation as today's other common usage words, such as CD-ROM, DVD, email, World Wide Web, and VCR.

Those loggers were not the rapers and pillagers of the land as many have chosen to portray them. By its very definition, rape means nonconsent. Our government encouraged, promoted, and yes, demanded the massive cutting of timber for wartime and postwar purposes. There was a job to be done. Everyone, including children collecting scrap metal and buying 25-cent war stamps, was expected to give their all in the war effort.

Our government pushed, begged, prodded, and pleaded with timber workers for greater lumber production. It was acknowledged that "conservation and proper forestry practices could be made up after the war..." Implied in this statement was the reality that if it came to pass we lost the War, the Japanese would not be receiving our lumber via importing our logs, they would have outright ownership of all our timberlands. If their effort to torch our forests had been successful, there can be little doubt they would now be logging the second growth.

It was the all-out production by loggers and mill workers that tipped the scales of war. The facts speak for themselves. Were it not for their

REFORESTATION
A tree planter rebuilds the landscape. The trees come from the Roseburg Forest Product Nursery. Photograph courtesy of Roseburg Forest Products.

blood, sweat, and tears we would have lost the war. It was Douglas fir that built the shipyards and airplane factories, the decking for escort aircraft carriers when teak was unavailable, dry docks for ship repairs, and warehouses. The list is endless.

Yet, as recently as 1998, the propaganda machine rolled on, fueled by backers of an Oregon ballot measure called Measure 64. This measure was so severe it was feared it would be the final nail driven in the timber industry's coffin. The measure went down in flames. The unsubstantiated propaganda and disinformation tossed out in support of this measure demonized "those who for the past 120 years have destroyed [Oregon's] resources for private profit." There is no arguing with the fact that each and everyone of us, our children, and our grandchildren are the profiteers of the massive logging that took place during two decades of such destruction. In the earlier years, a country was being built.

The Slaughter of the Scapegoats

Although damned, defiled, and treated like the paper in the bottom of the bird cage, the loggers of yesteryear served their country meritoriously at a time when our nation was threatened. No one could predict the outcome of World War II.

Working under inherently dangerous conditions, the timber workers' jobs were made more hazardous by fatigue brought on by mandated long hours. In battling the odds, hundreds paid with life and limb. Lest we forget, a good many of the men in the woods were not so enthralled with their jobs. They looked for a safer more gentle way to aid in the war effort. The Government in effect said, "No Way!"

According to the Oregon Department of Veterans' Affairs, between the years 1941 and 1955, which encompass WWII and the Korean War, 3,104 Oregon servicemen were killed.

According to Oregon's compilation of Work-Related Fatalities by Industry, during those same years 779 loggers and 231 sawmill workers were killed. This makes a total of 1,010 Oregon timber workers killed on the home front in their attempt to fulfill civilian and government needs. What other support industry and producer of war materials suffered one-third the number of casualties as that state's front line armed forces? For every three Oregon servicemen killed, one Oregon timber worker followed.

The timber industry's recorded deaths failed to take into account log haulers for the years 1943 and 1944. Since the war did not begin until December 1941, no loggers' deaths are listed for 1941; although, no doubt, at least several Oregon servicemen died at Pearl Harbor, and that number is included in the total armed forces casualty list.

Data is lacking for 1942 as to the number of Oregon logging or sawmill fatalities. In the absence of that statistic, the author used the next year's (1943) fatalities, which should be about the same, to arrive at the total timber industry deaths.

These figures do not take into account the walking wounded who have walked, and continue to walk, among us—some with shattered limbs that continue to ache and impede them in their daily lives.

Data is unavailable from Oregon as to the number of artificial members, such as arms, hands, legs, teeth and eyes, dispensed to timber workers for the subject years.

Posthumous Tribute

There was a war to be won, and paramount in everyone's mind was the winning of that war. The message of the times was that doomsday was just around the corner—not down the road a ways. Retired U.S. Air Force General Paul Tibbets, the pilot chosen to drop the Hiroshima bomb on Japan on August 6, 1945, said it best, "There is no second place in war."

The timber workers who played such a major role in WWII, the postwar recovery, and the Korean Conflict have been denied any form of recognition for their praise worthy sacrifices. An honored place in history is their due, not a dishonored legacy. In a very real sense, those men were heroes.

The loggers can be likened to our Vietnam veterans who were spit upon when they returned home, and the Korean War veterans who were all but forgotten. Like the Vietnam veterans, the loggers were proud of what they were doing while so engaged, but later found that they were looked down upon. They took it on the chin.

Although slow in coming, the veterans of these two wars have at last been recognized for their sacrifices. As late as 1996, some 43 years after the end of the Korean War, Oregon honored its Korean veterans with the dedication of a granite monument in Portland.

The space left void for any positive recognition of the timber workers and their communal efforts has been stuffed with distrust and censure.

During the latter war years, with much ado and a military band playing in the background, high military dignitaries or representatives of the War Production Board showed up at the very large lumber mills to honor the timber workers. These mills were the likes of Weyerhaeuser Timber Company and Willamette Industries.

At these ceremonies sterling silver, red, white, and blue "E" pins were either pinned on or handed to employees, management, and union representatives. With great fanfare, a color guard raised the Army/Navy "E" flag over the facilities. These awards were for outstanding contributions to the war effort.

At that moment in time, the government validated and paid tribute to these men.

But the owners and employees of small family-owned sawmills and the loggers toiling away in the woods were far from any ceremonies. No dignitaries came to their workplace symbolically handing out awards or commending them for a job well done.

All these men performed meritoriously and many paid a high price. Their only badges were the many scars they wore and continue to wear.

These men deserve the applause and respect of a grateful nation. And it is long overdue!

References

Personal Interviews

SUTHERLIN POLICE OFFICERS/CHIEFS:

Dave Pichette
Sutherlin Police force for 26 years—commencing 1947

Richard Crumal
Police Chief 1953-1971

Audie Campbell
Police force 1954-1957

Richard Schwartz
Chief of Police 1987-1993 (joined department 1965)

OAKLAND POLICE CHIEF:

Walter "Turk" Manning
Chief for 15 years (hired in 1952)

LOGGERS: VERIFICATION LOGGING/GAMBLING/SAWMILLS:

Dode Winter and Brothers "Bud" and Cliff

Bill Kenwisher
80+ year-old logger from Sutherlin area

Bert Baimbridge
Lifetime Douglas County resident and rancher

John Bratton
85-year-old logger now living in Medford area

OREGON HISTORIANS:

John McWade
Eugene, OR. Retired after 42 years with Oregon Department of Forestry: forestry rules regarding fire danger and low humidity shutdown of woods

William D. Hagenstein
Portland, OR. Consulting Forester, author, active and renown in the Society of American Foresters since 1938: regarding use of POWs during WWII, forestry practices and statistics

Bert Webber
Medford, OR. Author, editor, and publisher—Webb Research Group Publishers

COUNTY AND STATE AGENCIES/SERVICES:

Douglas County Law Library—research gambling laws

U. S. Department of Labor, Occupational Safety & Health Division—safety ratings

U.S. Veterans' Administration—statistics

U. S. Bureau of Labor Statistics
San Francisco, CA—CPI

Umpqua Regional Council of Governments
Roseburg—statistics

Oregon Workers Compensation Board, Research and Analysis Division, Salem, OR—statistics

Oregon Historical Society
Portland, OR—wartime Portland shipyards

OTHERS:

Anna Lou Allen
Daughter of proprietor of Jug's Club

Letha Nicolazzi Barnes
Recollection wartime shortages and women in sawmills

Doug Robertson
(1989) Douglas County Commissioner—statistics

Atty. James McGinty
City Atty of Myrtle Creek for 26 years; recently retired from private practice—regarding gambling and prostitution

Nancy Nichols Gallop
Daughter of early pioneer family—regarding ranchers burning of timber for pasture

Tom Gilman
Lifetime resident of Sutherlin, owner of Pacific Northwest Steel—consultant on sawmills and metals

Dwayne Linton
Resident of Sutherlin for over 40 yrs. and a business owner; active in civic affairs—regarding liquor laws and miscellaneous matters

Russell Lawson
Microbiology Instructor
San Joaquin Delta College, Stockton, CA—resource on syphilis

Jeanne Calvert
Grants Pass, OR, ex-wife of District Atttorney Robert Davis

Don O'Neil
Lifelong resident of Sutherlin—sawmills

References

NEWSPAPERS:

Sutherlin Sun
Sutherlin: 1940s and 1950s—miscellaneous history

Roseburg News Review
Roseburg, OR recent miscellaneous forestry matters

New York Times
1940s microfilm—wartime information

OTHER REFERENCES:

Archives of Weyerhaeuser Timber Company
Tacoma, WA

Douglas County Museum
Oral Histories (1940-50) of:
    (1) R. J. Duffy, restaurateur and bartender, Roseburg, OR; gambling, pay-offs, raids, and Oregon Liquor Laws, and
    (2) Albert Flegal, Roseburg business owner, Roseburg Mayor, Douglas Co. Commissioner, State Representatives and State Senator—prostitution and pay-offs

Ft. Lewis Military Museum
Ft. Lewis, WA—Use of POWs

Paul F. Ehinger & Associates
Eugene, OR. Consultants to the Forest Products Industry—Logging and sawmill statistics

Roseburg Forest Products
Roseburg—regarding Kenneth Ford

Ruralite Service, Inc.
Forest Grove, OR (2/80 issue)

BOOKS:

American Guide Series
Sponsored by Oregon State Board of Control, *Oregon: End of the Trail*, Published by Binfords & Mort 1951

Andrews, Ralph W.
This Was Logging, published by Superior Publishing Company 1954

Andrews, Ralph W.
Glory Days of Logging, published by Superior Publishing Company 1956

Jones, James
Bad Blood: The Tuskegee Experiment, published by Free Press, 1981 Ed.

Lucia, Ellis
Head Rig, Story of the West Coast Lumber Industry, published by Overland West Press 1965

Minter, Harold A.
Umpqua Valley Oregon and its Pioneers, published by Binfords & Mort 1967

Pierre, Joseph H.
When Timber Stood Tall, published by Superior Publishing Company 1979

Wackerman, Hagenstein & Michell
Harvesting Timber Crops, published by McGraw-Hill Book Company, 2nd Ed. 1966

Webber, Bert
Swivel-Chair Logger: The Life and Work of Anton A. "Tony" Lausman, published by YeGalleon Press 1976

Webber, Bert
Silent Siege III: Japanese Attacks on North America in World War II: Ships Sunk, Air Raids, Bombs Dropped, Civilians Killed: Documentary— published by YeGalleon Press 1992

Wentz, Walt
Bringing Out the Big Ones, published by Oregon Forest Products Association 1983

HELLGATE PRESS

WIDOW-MAKERS & RHODODENDRONS
LOGGERS—THE UNSUNG HEROES OF WORLD WAR II

DORIS WINTER HUBBARD

WELCOME TO
HELLGATE PRESS

If you enjoyed reading Widow-Makers & Rhododendrons, do something nice for your friends: Order copies for them, today.

Hellgate Press is named after the historic and rugged Hellgate Canyon on southern Oregon's scenic Rogue River. The raging river that flows below the canyon's towering jagged cliffs has always attracted a special sort of individual—someone who seeks adventure. From the pioneers who bravely pursued the lush valleys beyond, to the anglers and rafters who take on its roaring challenges today, Hellgate Press publishes books that reflect this adventurous spirit. Our books are about military history, adventure travel, and outdoor recreation. On the following pages, we would like to introduce you to some of our latest titles and encourage you to join in the celebration of this unique spirit.

Walking Away From The Third Reich

The Experiences of a Teenager in Hitler's Army
by Claus W. Sellier

ISBN: 1-55571-513-3
308 pages, Paperback: $15.95

Seventeen-year-old boys are the same everywhere. This is a gripping story of a well-to-do German boy who is eager to serve, but learns the hard way that war is not a game. From the shelter of his private boys' school, to the devastating battle fields of Germany, he learns what is truly important to him.

Immigrant Soldier

From the Baltics to Vietnam
by Vic Pakis

ISBN: 1-55571-512-5
240 pages, Paperback: $15.95

The story of a family whose fortunes changed dramatically due to the rise of Communism and Nazism and a flight for freedom to the United States. A son describes his family's experiences as they flee Latvia, and how he joins the U.S. Army to fight against Communism and oppression in Southeast Asia.

Survival

Diary of an American POW in World War II
by Samuel G. Higgins

ISBN: 1-55571-514-1
228 pages, Paperback: $14.95

A patriotic southerner joins the army and is captured in one of the most intense battles of WWII. During his three-month incarceration in the infamous Stalag IXB, he secretly made notes in the margins of his Bible. Fifty years later, the hundreds of entries trigger recollections of the outrage he felt, the squalid living conditions, the treatment of the Jewish prisoners, and the starvation and death that surrounded him. It is a testament to what the human spirit can endure.

Look for Hellgate Press books in your favorite bookstore, or order by calling 1-800-228-2275 or online at *www.psi-research.com/hellgate.htm*

Order Direct
FROM HELLGATE PRESS

To order any of our books direct, simply complete the order and payment information below and send to:

Hellgate Press, P.O. Box 3727 Central Point, OR 97502-0032

or call us at 1-800-228-2275 (International orders, call 1-541-479-9464) or fax this completed form to 1-541-476-1479.

Title	Price	Quantity	Cost
Army Museums: West of the Mississippi	$17.95		
Byron's War: I never will be young again... (hardbound edition)	$21.95		
Gulf War Debriefing Book: An After Action Report	$18.95		
From Hiroshima With Love	$18.95		
Keeping Australia on the Left: A Catamaran Odyssey Around Australia	$13.95		
Legacy of Leadership: Lessons from Admiral Lord Nelson (hardbound edition)	$17.95		
Night Landing: A Short History of West Coast Smuggling	$13.95		
Order of Battle: Allied Ground Forces of Operation Desert Storm	$17.95		
Pilots, Man Your Planes!: A History of Naval Aviation (hardbound edition)	$33.95		
Rebirth of Freedom: From Nazis and Communists to a New Life in America	$16.95		
Regret to Inform You: Experiences of Families Who Lost a Family Member in Vietnam	$16.95		
The War That Would Not End: U.S. Marines in Vietnam, 1971–1973	$19.95		
This Woman's Army: The Dynamics of Sex and Violence in the Military	$16.95		
Words of War: From Antiquity to Modern Times	$13.95		
Widow-Makers & Rhododendrens	$19.95		
Memories Series			
K-9 Soldiers: Vietnam and After	$13.95		
After The Storm: A Vietnam Veteran's Reflection	$14.95		
Green Hell: The Battle for Guadalcanal	$18.95		
Immigrant Soldier: From the Baltics to Vietnam	$15.95		
Oh, What A Lovely War!	$10.95		
Project Omega: Eye of the Beast	$13.95		
Survival: Diary of an American POW in World War II	$14.95		
Through My Eyes: 91st Infantry Division, Italian Campaign 1942–1945	$14.95		
Walking Away From the Third Reich: Experiences of a Teenager in Hitler's Army	$15.95		
Where Duty Calls: Growing Up in the Marine Corps	$12.95		
		Subtotal	$
		Shipping	$
		Grand Total	$

Ordering Information
Street address:

Name:

Address:

City: State: Zip:

Daytime Phone: Email:

Ship To
If different than above:

Name:

Address:

City: State: Zip:

Daytime Phone: ☐ Check if this is a gift

Payment Information

☐ **Check** (Make payable to PSI Research)   **Charge:** ☐ VISA ☐ MasterCard ☐ AMEX ☐ Discover

Card Number: Expires:

Signature: Name on Card:

Phone orders accepted Monday through Friday, 6:30 AM to 5:00 PM (Pacific). Please have your credit card and order information available.

You may fax orders 24 hours-a-day. If a transmission problem occurs, please mark your second fax as a duplicate.

International Orders
We are happy to take international orders; however, all shipments outside of the U.S. must have the proper international delivery charge included on an international money order. For more information, please call 1 (541) 479-9464

Shipping
We ship regular UPS Ground; however, rush service is available. Please call for additional information and pricing.

Return Policy
If you're not completely satisfied, please return any item within 15 days of purchase for a prompt refund (except shipping & handling). Please explain your reason for returning the item and enclose your packing slip to ensure proper processing.

Shipping Chart:
If your purchase is: U.S.A. Shipping:

$0-25	$5.00
$25.01 – $50	$6.00
$50.01 – $100	$7.00
$100.01 – $175	$9.00
$175.01 – $250	$13.00
$250.01 – $500	$18.00
$500.01 +	4% of total

Visit us online
To learn more about Hellgate Press or to order any of our titles online, visit our Website at: **http://www.psi-research.com/hellgate.htm**

If you have any questions or need assistance, you may email us at: **info@psi-research.com**